DANCING IN THE GARDEN OF THE LOTUS SUTRA

DANCING IN THE GARDEN OF THE LOTUS SUTRA

The Three Gates To Freedom From
Alcohol Addiction

MARGARET CRAM-HOWIE

Foreword by
KANJIN CEDERMAN SHONIN

Columbus, Ohio

Dancing in the Garden of the Lotus Sutra:
THE THREE GATES TO FREEDOM FROM
ALCOHOL ADDICTION

Published by Gatekeeper Press
3971 Hoover Rd. Suite 77
Columbus, OH 43123-2839
www.GatekeeperPress.com

ISBN: 9781619847897
eISBN: 9781619847903

Printed in the United States of America

CONTENTS

Foreword.. vii

Preface.. xi

The First Gate: Awareness

Chapter One: Lifting The Veil Of Delusion 3

Chapter Two: Discovering Your Buddha Nature 17

Chapter Three: Taking Refuge 31

The Second Gate: Introspection

Chapter Four: The Precepts.................................... 45

Chapter Five: Planting The Roots Of Virtue.................... 59

Chapter Six: Atonement 75

The Third Gate: The Dance Of Life

Chapter Seven: Flow 87

Chapter Eight: Prayer And Meditation............................ 97

Chapter Nine: Opening The Mind And Heart
To Love.. 109

Works Cited.. 113

FOREWORD

This book has been a great journey for "Myosho" Margaret Cram-Howie. When I first met Margaret, she was a soft-spoken quiet lady interested in Buddhism and how it could change people's lives through the Lotus Sutra. Over the many years that we have learned and trained together, I was able to experience her immense strength and fortitude in pursuing the purpose of a good life and her sincere wish to help all suffering beings. Since then she has continued on the path and now shares her teaching with her readers in *Dancing in the Garden of the Lotus Sutra*. It is in the birth of a great Lotus Flower in the pond of the world of suffering beings that we are able to see strength and fortitude in the midst of suffering and that there is genuine hope for everyone.

Through this journey of self-reflection, she imparts to the reader many great treasures of the Buddha's teachings that she has received and implemented on her path. As of now, there has been no one that I feel has utilized and shared the Lotus Sutra in the scope of addiction recovery. This book seems to focus on the recovery from alcohol but it is too great a vehicle to be minimized to one subject because it can be applied to any imbalance in our lives and gifts us with tools to change. I know that a great many people will awaken from the world of delusion and leave the realm of suffering to enter the Pure Land of Mt. Sacred Eagle, which is right before us in our lives if we just put down the drink of delusion and choose enlightenment over death and suffering.

In honor of this important occasion, I would like to offer a prayer for all who are fearless and take the next step to a beautiful life by contemplating this book:

Honor be to the Buddha

Honor be to our Founder Nichiren Shonin

Honor be to the Lotus Sutra of the Wonderful Dharma

Honor be to the protective deities of the Dharma

Through this great work, we dedicate its merit to the countless suffering beings dealing with addiction. May they be able to realize their Buddha-nature and quickly become Buddhas in this life. May this offering benefit Beings of the ten directions and help them to fully realize their potential and strength through wisdom and compassion. May all that meet this teaching realize their original nature and be able to benefit others with their experience and teaching, to create a beautiful Pure Land here and now.

Namu Myoho Renge Kyo
With Gassho, Kanjin Cederman Shonin
Head Priest of Seattle Choeizan Enkyoji Temple

PREFACE

This book will guide you along a path. The path begins with recovery from addiction and gently leads you into a life of joy where you learn, moment by moment, to dance with whatever is present in your life. This is the path I traveled.

I first sobered up in the mid-seventies. My life changed quickly for the better. I returned to university, started my career, fell in love and started our family. But I wasn't able to remain sober. When difficulties hit, as is normal in this human life, I did not have the necessary skills to deal with them. I felt confused and alone. I felt trapped and helpless. I turned once again to the bottle.

One night, after a few drinks with a longtime friend, she surprised and shocked me and shook me out of my complacency. She told me it was clear that I had a problem and that drinking wasn't going to help it. She encouraged me to get professional help for whatever was causing my sadness. Then she said that neither she, nor anyone else she knew, preferred me drunk to sober. She asked me to give up booze and become sober again.

I am one of the lucky ones who returned to sobriety after a relapse. I am living proof that it is possible. I now have over thirty-two years of continuous sobriety. If you relapse during your recovery, learn from it and carry on. It is simply one of the steps along your path.

The steps along the path in this book are loosely based on the principles I extracted from The Twelve Steps of Alcoholics Anonymous. I started my recovery journey in the rooms of AA. The primary difference between the twelve steps as presented in this book and the official twelve steps of Alcoholics Anonymous is that there is no mention of a god of any understanding in the steps along the path presented in this book. I never believed in an external god of any description and this was problematic for me in making sense of the steps. I hear from many others in recovery that the issue of the word "god" in the twelve-step programs is a problem for them too. For some, this problem keeps them away from recovery programs. It is my hope that this book will be of help to those addicts who want the principles of recovery without committing to a god.

I met several teachers/mentors along the way. I studied with Marshall Rosenberg and learned the gentleness and wisdom of Nonviolent Communication. I studied with Dr. Deepak Chopra and became a certified meditation teacher with The Chopra Center. I blossomed in the garden of the Lotus Sutra, studying and practicing with my Buddhist minister, my sensei Reverend Kanjin Cederman. It is in the beautiful stories, parables, and teachings of Nichiren Shu Buddhism that I find the fullness of life. It is my hope that by sharing my path, you may also find a passage out of addiction and into joyfulness.

My life is woven with the texture of many teachings. It is interpreted from many different perspectives dependent on the role(s) I play at various stages of my life. At times I am influenced primarily by my role as mother, at others by my role as wife, at others by my role as teacher, and on and on. It shifts and morphs as I live my life.

I now understand that everything in life is interconnected. One strand in the tapestry of life might emphasize a spiritual component, another a mental component, another a physical component, another an emotional component and yet another a social component. Each strand, each component, affects the completed tapestry. All have a role to play. The spiritual component for each step in this book is illustrated by telling a Buddhist story. Other components (mental, physical, emotional, social) are drawn from a variety of sources.

The path, the journey out of addiction, is divided into three sections. Each section is entered through a gate. The first gate is the gate of awareness. The second gate is the gate of introspection. The third gate is the gate that leads you into the garden of the Lotus Sutra where you learn to dance with impermanence.

THE FIRST GATE
AWARENESS

BUDDHA AND HELL

Suppose we ask where the Buddha is and where hell is. Some sutras state that hell is below the earth, while others state that the Pure Land of Buddhas is in the west. But the explicit truth is that both hell and Buddha exist within five feet of our bodies.

(Nichiren's writings: January 5, 1281, 58 years old, at Minobu, *Showa Teihon*, p. 1856)

Chapter One

LIFTING THE VEIL
OF DELUSION

The first step in Alcoholics Anonymous reads, "We admitted we were powerless over alcohol – that our lives had become unmanageable." This step brings awareness to two things: 1) that the alcoholic is powerless over alcohol, and 2) that the alcoholic's life is unmanageable. The active alcoholic does not recognize this description of his/her life. The active alcoholic is in denial, seeing life through the veil of delusion. In some cases the veil of delusion is a heavy curtain.

In Buddhist philosophy it is Mara, the deceiver, who weaves this veil. Mara is seen both as a being in the world and as a metaphor. Mara represents feelings and thoughts that lead us away from our natural, healthy existence, our Buddha Nature. It is Mara who approaches Siddhartha as he sits under the Bodhi tree seeking enlightenment.

Being a crafty fellow, Mara brings his three daughters

to tempt Siddhartha. He tries to turn Siddhartha away from his quest for enlightenment. The first daughter to approach Siddhartha represents attraction or craving. Mara's second daughter represents boredom or aversion. The third daughter represents passions that ensnare and delude us. These three temptations can draw almost any human away from a healthy path. But Mara's daughters fail to entice Siddhartha and he transforms into the Buddha, the Enlightened One. This is a story of hope for all of humankind, especially addicts.

Every alcoholic knows these three temptations well. Craving, boredom, and passions that ensnare are common stock among alcoholics. These are the temptations that keep the alcoholic lost in addiction, viewing life through the veil of delusion. It is this veil that obscures reality and allows the alcoholic to believe his/her life is normal. Cravings, boredom, and passions that ensnare are the powerful temptations that keep the alcoholic returning to the bottle. Once the alcoholic drinks alcohol, i.e. engages in his/her addiction, thoughts and behaviors shift and become problematic. There are problems at home or with friends or at work. You get it. Life is unmanageable.

At twenty-four years old, my life appeared to be not going in the direction I wanted. I dropped out of university. My roommates asked me to move out and I moved back home with my parents. In short order they asked me to move out too. I moved to a new city, believing I could make a fresh start. I met with a psychiatrist to ensure that this new beginning would work. From my perspective, life was throwing me some tough situations and I believed alcohol helped me deal with my life. I often said, "If you had my life, you would drink too." My psychiatrist challenged that belief. He said I had it backwards. He claimed the tough situations were a result of my drinking. He challenged me to give up drinking for two weeks and see what would happen.

Determined to prove him wrong, I accepted the challenge. To my horror, I discovered I wasn't able to give up alcohol. The craving was too intense. I experienced the first shattering of the delusional world I believed in at the time. If you still believe alcohol is your friend, I challenge you to give it up for two weeks and see what happens.

The temptations that keep us caught in the delusional world of addiction are craving, boredom, and passions that ensnare. Craving is a major problem in early recovery. It was a huge hurdle for me. Let's look at it first. I was fifteen when I tasted alcohol for the first time but I remember that experience vividly. It burned going down my throat and exploded in the center of my being, enveloping me in a sense of personal power and skill that I had never known before. I chased that feeling for ten years. I craved alcohol and believed it would give me that euphoria again. The delusion is that the alcoholic high is real, that it is repeatable, and that it is the answer to life's problems. The craving I'd developed over my ten-year drinking period left me powerless to the grips of alcohol. I knew I couldn't beat it on my own and signed myself into a treatment center. It was 1975.

Craving is really a form of anxiety. It consists of racing thoughts, where the rate of your thoughts speeds up. It is not unusual to string catastrophic thoughts together. What if this happens? What if that happens? Anxiety will often have a physical component as well. This could be expressed by an inability to sit still. The next time you experience craving, bring awareness of what is happening to your thoughts and to your body. If you notice thoughts flying around in your mind at lightning speed, or if you are pacing the floor or tapping your fingers on a table, you can be sure Mara's first daughter, Craving, is looking for a way in. To keep her out, use a thought-stopping technique. Try this brief meditation technique I learned at The Chopra Center: Take a deep breath in, filling your chest and your belly. As you take the breath in, silently say "So." Then exhale the breath as slowly as possible. On the exhalation, silently say "Hum." Repeat this "So-Hum" meditation while you continue to breathe in fully and exhale slowly. Repeating the "So-Hum" mantra will help stop your racing thoughts and matching it to your breath and slowing your breath will naturally calm your entire body.

If your craving for alcohol persists, you may require a life interruption like I did by going to a treatment or drug rehabilitation center. Not every alcoholic requires treatment, but it was a valuable experience for me. At the treatment center I attended, I took a drug called Antabuse. Antabuse is the common name for the prescription drug, disulfiram. At the rehabilitation center I went to in the mid-seventies, everyone was given Antabuse. That is no longer the case, but some rehabilitation centers do prescribe it to select clients.

Antabuse does not take cravings away, but it acts as a poison in your body if you drink alcohol when you are on it. It causes severe pain and in some incidents even causes death. The warnings I received about what would happen to me if I mixed alcohol with Antabuse were enough to scare me into not drinking. Clearly I would not get what I was seeking from alcohol if I took Antabuse. I stayed on Antabuse while in treatment and for several months after I left treatment. During the time I was taking Antabuse, I was able to learn other techniques to manage cravings.

One of the techniques I learned in treatment goes by the acronym "HALT." Each letter stands for something that can easily trigger cravings: Hungry, Angry, Lonely, and Tired. If you notice you are hungry, find something to eat. Keep fresh fruit and healthy snacks on hand so you can grab something quickly. If you allow hunger to grow, it will invite craving in.

If you become aware of angry feelings, do a walking meditation. It is helpful to keep the body moving when the emotions are fired up. Find a space free of clutter: a hallway in your apartment, or a stretch of grass in your backyard. Take off your shoes and socks and feel the ground beneath your feet. Cast your gaze a few steps in front of you. Slowly raise one foot, lifting the heel first and gradually rolling forward to your toes. Place your foot down a short distance ahead, again being aware of your heel connecting to the ground first, followed by your instep and toes. Raise your other foot and follow the same procedure. Allow your angry thoughts to fly around and away as you focus your attention on your feet as they ground you to the earth below, the earth that supports you. Continue for ten minutes or more.

If you notice you are feeling lonely, try to connect with someone. Maybe you have a recovery buddy or a therapist. Phone or text them and chat a bit. Even if you don't tell them how you are feeling, your loneliness will lessen. Go to a space where there are other people, maybe a mall or a coffee shop or the library. Just being around other people is often helpful. If you have a dog, take him out for a walk or play fetch with him.

If you are tired, take a nap. Then learn and implement a sleep regimen to combat tiredness. Go to bed at the same time every night and get up at the same time each morning. Aim for a minimum of seven to eight hours of sleep every night. Have a warm bath or drink a cup of warm milk a half hour before your bedtime. Then crawl into bed and read something inspirational till lights-out time. Keep your bedroom dark and quiet.

Awareness of triggers for craving is a key component to staying sober in early recovery. Once you are managing your cravings and staying sober for periods of time, it is likely you will be visited by Mara's second daughter. She will whisper in your ear that this sober life is not worth all the effort it takes. She will mock your efforts and tell you that you have become boring, that your life is ordinary. Be on the lookout for her voice in your head. Remember she is a temptress. Awareness is again the key. Start to pay attention to your thoughts. Ask yourself, "Do I really believe this?" and "Is this really true?" Write down some of your troubling thoughts about your new life. Read them again twenty-four hours later and see if they still hold power with you or whether they have disappeared. My experience is that most of my troubling thoughts disappear within twenty-four hours. The trick is to get them out of your head by writing them down and then letting them go for twenty-four hours.

Mara's second daughter is quickly followed by the third. If Mara's second daughter can convince you that your sober life is boring, then it is much easier for the third daughter to tempt you with passions that ensnare and delude you. This is where cross addiction or dual addiction can enter your life. You convince yourself that because you are not drinking, other behaviors are okay. You may turn to gambling, overeating, online pornography, serial sexual encounters, or ANY behavior that is compulsive and leads you into another form of addiction.

I cannot speak from personal experience. I am one of the lucky ones that did not go down this road. However, I watched several friends and recovery buddies fall into this trap. Passion, in and of itself, is not the problem. There is healthy passion that drives a person to pursue a career, or reach an athletic goal, or enjoy a hobby. Mara's daughter will tempt you with a passion, a desire that ensnares you. The longer you engage with this passion, this object of desire, the more you become ensnared. The binding becomes tighter and tighter and fear emerges. Mara's domain is one of desire coupled with fear. Healthy passion/healthy desire gives you a sense of expansion, of freedom, of energy. Be mindful of your pursuits in early recovery. Do you start with a burst of energy and excitement that is followed by lethargy, fear, and secrecy? If so, there is a good chance you have succumbed to the passion that ensnares – the trademark of Mara's third daughter.

The light of awareness helps you to understand what it means for an alcoholic to be powerless over alcohol. When active in alcoholic drinking, you are unaware of the many triggers or situations that create craving, that elusive voice that tells you everything would be better if you just had a drink. And, once you have that first drink, you are powerless over what happens next. Taking that first drink is what makes an alcoholic's life unmanageable. It's not the third drink, or the seventh drink, or the fourteenth drink. It's the first drink!

There is one situation in particular that brought this home for me. I'd just finished my last exam and my last shift at work on the same day. It had been a hard year for me – full-time classes during the day followed by a full-time job in the evenings. I'd worked hard and was ready for some time off. I celebrated by going out for a few drinks with some girlfriends. I remember going to the bar and ordering the first round of drinks. My next memory was waking up in a hospital bed with my leg in traction and no idea how I got there. It was a terrifying experience. I questioned the nurses and eventually put the story together. While crossing a street, a car ran into me. That is the only detail I know.

That one detail is all I know about that evening. I

blacked out – an alcohol-induced memory loss. It wasn't how I thought the evening would go when I sat down to celebrate with my friends. While I was in treatment, I looked back at my drinking experiences. It wasn't unusual for me to plan to have just a glass of wine with a meal and then drink the whole bottle. It wasn't unusual for me to stop in the bar for "a" drink with friends and then be kicked out at closing time. It was never my intention to get drunk! And it didn't always happen. Because I did sometimes have just that one glass of wine, or that one drink with friends, I thought I was in control. I was puzzled, and scared, and embarrassed when my drinking was out of control, but I convinced myself that it was the exception. I allowed the veil of delusion to obscure the reality that my life had become unmanageable.

Is your life unmanageable? Do you plan to stop by for one drink and end up staying till the bar closes? Do you miss family time because you are drinking? Are you late for work because you are hung over? Have you lost a relationship due to your drinking? Have you lost a job due to your drinking? Are you spending money you can't afford on your drinking? Do you think you can control your drinking?

The only people I know who try to control their drinking are alcoholics. Because that veil of delusion is so effective at fooling us about what is real, I suggest you keep a journal. Every time you have a drink, write in your journal first. What is your intention? What do you think is going to happen? When the drinking episode is over, write in your journal again. What actually happened? Write it down. It is much harder to trick yourself if you journal every day. Every day, write down if you had a drink or not, what your intention was, and what actually happened. You may discover a pattern. You may not. Either way, you will see your life more clearly.

If you are powerless over alcohol, it is because of that first drink. That first drink is the end result of thoughts and feelings that set up craving. Becoming aware of your actual drinking pattern and the precursors to craving gives you the freedom to make a choice.

If you decide you want to quit drinking, see a medical doctor first and discuss your options. You may require medical detox. I served for several years on the Board of Directors for our local detox center. Find out if there is a similar facility in your city. You may want to discuss using Antabuse or one of the newer drugs that reduce cravings. These are decisions to make with your doctor.

Start trying out the strategies/techniques presented in this chapter:

1. Thought-stopping using the "So-Hum" meditation

2. Eating regularly

3. Walking meditation to lessen angry thoughts

4. Connecting with a "recovery buddy"

5. Establishing a sleep routine

6. Challenging your thoughts by asking, "Do I really believe this?"

7. Writing down your bothersome thoughts and letting them go for twenty-four hours

8. Journaling your drinking episodes and intentions

Early recovery can be a very stressful time. To relieve that stress and, at the same time, become aware of how stress is affecting your body, I recommend you try Progressive Muscle Relaxation. When I first sobered up, I didn't know how to relax. I didn't know that I clenched my jaw, that I tapped my foot whenever I sat down, that I thrashed around in my bed when I slept. I didn't know the difference between being tense and being relaxed. But I did have the good fortune to be around people who could see the physical tension I was unable to even recognize, and these people guided me.

One extremely useful item I was given was a cassette tape (remember, this was the mid-seventies) that taught body awareness and progressive muscle relaxation. I still have the original tape. It is called *Self-Relaxation Training*, by Sherwin B. Coulter and Julio J. Guerra. The tape was made in 1976. Similar items could easily be found online today. Simply search "progressive muscle relaxation" and you will find many useful resources. I found it useful to play the tape until I learned how to do this relaxation technique on my own. I did not possess enough focus to complete the entire procedure on my own. If you are unable to find a recording that works for you, I suggest you make your own.

Progressive Muscle Relaxation Meditation

Sitting in a reclining chair works well, but sitting anywhere that you are comfortable is fine. Feel free to use pillows and/or blankets as props. You can even lie down. Wear loose clothing and remove your shoes. Set aside about fifteen minutes to complete the exercise. Choose a spot where you won't be disturbed. Turn off your phone.

Take a deep breath in, hold it for five seconds, and then let it go. On your next breath, tighten the muscles in your toes. This usually involves flexing them downwards, but whatever works for you. Hold the breath for five seconds and focus on tensing the muscles in your toes. Notice how it feels. Release the breath and relax the muscles in your toes. Notice how these muscles feel now. Breathe normally. When you are ready, move your focus to the next muscle group, moving up your body. You might choose your entire foot, or move to your ankle. Again, take a deep breath in and tense the muscles in the chosen area. Hold the breath for five seconds while you hold the muscles tense and notice how it feels. Release the breath and simultaneously release the muscles. Notice how the relaxed muscles feel. Continue in this manner, working your way up the body: thighs, hips, stomach, back, arms, shoulders, jaw, nose, forehead.

Do this exercise at least once a day, slowly tensing each muscle group on the in-breath and then slowly relaxing each muscle group on the out-breath. You will become more aware of the muscle groups that make up your body and you will be able to differentiate various physical sensations in your body. As your body awareness increases you will become more grounded. As you become more and more adept at recognizing signs of tension/stress in your body and how to relieve that tension, you will become less susceptible to physical cravings and physical symptoms of anxiety.

This first step into awareness is a big one. Give yourself a pat on the back. You are stepping into recovery from your addiction.

Chapter Two

DISCOVERING YOUR BUDDHA NATURE

The second step along the recovery path will shine awareness in two areas: 1) showing us the distinction between our ego selves and our Buddha Nature, and 2) recognizing that by cultivating our Buddha Nature, we automatically restore sanity in our lives. The traditional AA version of the second step reads, "Came to believe that a Power greater than myself could restore me to sanity." When I first approached sobriety, I considered myself to be an atheist. I made it through the first step and accepted that my life was unmanageable. I was looking forward to getting back a manageable life, to feeling some sense of personal power, some sense of accomplishment. And then I was hit with Step Two and that ominous uppercase "P" on "Power." I was told that this Power did not have to be God or even god. It could be anything as long as it wasn't me! This was a major problem for me when I first entered a twelve-step program and it remained a problem for years. I tried to follow a Christian path, but it didn't really make sense to me. I did start to have what I considered to be spiritual experiences. But I quickly came to realize that the source of these experiences was coming from somewhere inside myself, not from a god outside myself.

The discrepancy between what I was being told in twelve-step programs and what I was personally experiencing finally became reconciled when I began to study Nichiren Shu Buddhism. The concept is actually very simple. The "Power" is my "Buddha Nature." This power is within each of us. There is a "Buddha Nature" within me. There is a "Buddha Nature" within you. It is our original nature. We are born with it. The reference to "myself" is pointing to ego-self. In recovery, we need to look for help beyond our ego-selves, that serves only our self-interest, and instead cultivate our "Buddha Nature," that connects and aligns us with all other beings.

The Lotus Sutra is the primary text that Nichiren Shu Buddhists study. There is a story in Chapter 8 of *The Lotus Sutra* that helps illustrate this idea of going beyond our ego-selves and polishing the gem of our "Buddha Nature." When we polish the gem of our "Buddha Nature" we see it more clearly. This story is referred to as The Parable of The Hidden Gem. The story begins by introducing us to a poor man. He is dressed in rags and is wandering around the countryside. One day, he decides to visit a friend. His friend is very wealthy. The friend welcomes him and they enjoy an evening together filled with good food and wine. The poor man drinks one glass of wine after another and eventually passes out. The next morning, the wealthy man must leave on business before his poor friend wakes up. The wealthy man wants to help his friend so he sews a precious gem into the lining of the poor man's clothing. He imagines that his friend will find the gem and be able to live a comfortable life. However, the poor man awakens and is not aware of the hidden gem. He leaves his friend's house and continues to wander the countryside, barely able to earn enough for food and shelter. Years later the two friends meet again. The wealthy man cannot believe that his friend is still wandering around in rags. He asks how this could be since he left his friend a gem that would provide him with a comfortable life. The poor man asks, "What gem?" He is not aware of the gem hidden in the lining of his clothes until his friend shows it to him.

This story is called a parable because it is used to illustrate a spiritual lesson. The poor man is each of us before we realize our hidden gem, our "Buddha Nature" that exists within each of us. Without awareness it will remain hidden. The wealthy friend is the Buddha who has given each of us this precious gift that can remove suffering and provide ease in our world. As long as we wander around in a drunken state, a state of unawareness, nothing will change. We remain lost in the world of the Ego.

Our Ego world is concerned only with our physical body and our physical world. Think of the various labels we might apply to ourselves if asked the question, "Who are you?" Maybe you would answer that you are a mother, or a Canadian, or a teacher. These are labels that apply to me. What are some of the labels you would use? These labels come from your Ego world. They do not reflect your essential self. They change over time. It is also from the Ego world that our judgments of self and others arise: I'm too tall. She's not very pretty. My neighbor is a jerk! The critical Ego voice goes on and on.

The second step along the recovery path is asking us to let go of this critical, ego-focused voice and embrace our true nature, our "Buddha Nature." It is by polishing this stone, this gem, that we will be restored to sanity. Our "Buddha Nature" is our true essence, which is identical to the true essence of all beings. When we are in touch with our "Buddha Nature," we feel connected to all of life. We are content and see our place in the world. We are connected to all other beings and feel a sense of belonging. We start to value ourselves, and others, through our awareness of our "Buddha Nature."

So, how do we polish this stone, this gem, and bring out our "Buddha Nature"? Nichiren Daishonin states in *Showa Teihon*, p.1433, "A singing bird in a cage attracts uncaged birds, and the sight of these uncaged birds will make the caged birds want to be free. Likewise, the chanting of Odaimoku will bring out the Buddha nature within ourselves."

Chanting the Odaimoku is the primary practice of Nichiren Shu Buddhism. "Odaimoku" translates as "great" (O), "title" (dai), and "chant" (moku). The chanting of the Odaimoku is made up of the characters, "Namu Myoho Renge Kyo." "Namu" is derived from a Sanskrit word meaning "I honor" or "I give reverence to." Together it translates to "I give reverence to the Lotus Sutra." The Lotus

Sutra is the title of our primary text. Make it a practice to start each day by chanting the Odaimoku aloud a minimum of three times. "Namu Myoho Renge Kyo, Namu Myoho Renge Kyo, Namu Myoho Renge Kyo." This is the starting place for becoming aware of and growing the Buddha seed that exists within you. As you become more comfortable with your chanting, increase the number of repetitions.

Chanting the Odaimoku is a form of mantra meditation. I was first introduced to mantra meditation many years ago as a teenager. My girlfriend and I attended an information session on Transcendental Meditation and went on to learn this meditation technique and receive our mantras. This was in the 1960s. The Beatles had recently burst onto the music scene and they were students of Transcendental Meditation with Maharishi Mahesh Yogi. I confess I was more interested in following in the Beatles' footsteps than I was in meditation. However, my meditation practice soon became my primary focus as I began to experience its benefits.

Transcendental Meditation is a form of silent meditation, and involves repeating a sound known as a mantra. A mantra is important for its vibrational quality. The proper mantra has the ability to assist you to sink into your essential being. I was aware that something beyond my understanding was happening when I meditated but, in spite of that, I meditated only occasionally.

Then, in early recovery, someone gave me a copy of the book *The Relaxation Response* by Herbert Benson. Over the years it has become a bit of a classic in the field of stress management. I still have my original copy and refer to it from time to time. If you like to read and learn easily in this manner I recommend you get a copy, either at a used book store or online using Amazon. The premise behind this book is that you can create a "relaxation response" to counter the "fight or flight response" that your body automatically enters into when you perceive yourself to be in danger. The really fascinating piece is that the author chose as his study group a number of people who were practicing Transcendental Meditation. He found that each of the markers for the "fight or flight response" was reduced when his study group engaged in Transcendental Meditation! The author writes, "Our main purpose, however, is to discuss the Relaxation Response, for it may have a profound influence on your ability to deal with difficult situations and on the prevention and treatment of high blood pressure and its related, widespread diseases including heart attacks and strokes" (p.26, *The Relaxation Response*).

Early recovery certainly qualifies as a difficult situation that produces stress in the recovering alcoholic. Reading this book in my early days of recovery put me back on the path of Transcendental Meditation. I have studied and practiced many forms of meditation since then, but the most powerful, effective, and easiest to learn have all been mantra meditations. I studied with Dr. Deepak Chopra at The Chopra Center in Carlsbad, California and became a certified Primordial Sound Meditation teacher. Like Transcendental Meditation, it too is a form of silent, mantra-based meditation.

Chanting the Odaimoku retains all the qualities and

benefits of these silent, mantra-based meditations but adds the power of your voice. Clearly the spoken word is more powerful than the silent one. Chanting a mantra (the Odaimoku) aloud has a stronger vibrational effect than a silent repetition of a mantra. And the profound experience of chanting the Odaimoku together in a large group is beyond my ability to describe. My hope is that you will follow this path with me and experience it firsthand yourself.

Chanting the Odaimoku will naturally put you in touch with your "Buddha Nature" and that experience will, over time, restore you to sanity. You are able to tap into your original essence of connection and bring that experience back into your everyday life. Some forms of meditation are very useful at relieving a particular problem. An example would be the walking meditation to relieve feelings of anger, as we discussed in Chapter One. Other types of meditation will be taught throughout this book, when they meet a particular need. Meditation can fulfill a very specific purpose. However, mantra meditation is not designed to alleviate a specific situation or feeling. It is designed to grow our "Buddha Nature" so that there is less room for troublesome feelings, thus restoring us to sanity.

Let's take a closer look at this word sanity. Being restored to sanity implies that we were insane. This was not a difficult concept for me to grasp given that I spent time in psychiatric wards prior to sobering up. I have not required any psychiatric visits during my sobriety. Interesting. Most alcoholics in early recovery do not embrace the idea that they were insane. For most alcoholics, insanity conjures up images that are laced with fear and confusion. This was true when I first sobered up in the 1970s, and unfortunately it remains true today. In our current North American culture, there is a lack of understanding and acceptance of mental health issues.

Let's examine this scary word insanity. It is considered to be the opposite of sanity, so let's start there. Webster's dictionary defines sanity as "soundness of judgment, rational conduct." In Buddhist terms, one could say "right or skillful thinking" and "right or skillful action." Insanity is simply the absence of sound judgment, the absence of skillful thinking and/or skillful action. Not too scary. We have all made decisions or engaged in activities which we regretted. We have moments of insane (unskillful) thinking and we have moments of sane (skillful) thinking. These descriptors help us see the ebb and flow of our thoughts and our actions. Sanity and insanity are fluid concepts, not permanent labels. This second step asks you to consciously engage in more skillful thoughts and actions. It is a learning process and it takes time. Be gentle with yourself as you learn new ways of thinking and acting.

Acting in skillful ways causes happy results. Acting in unskillful ways causes unhappy results. Recovery from addiction is all about learning how to make skillful choices – making more sane choices than insane choices. It is often said around AA recovery tables that insanity is doing the same thing over and over and expecting different results.

Addiction recovery is a path, a journey. In our first step, we realized that our addiction put us on a path to an unmanageable life. The second step on the recovery path, like the Buddhist path, is made up of countless choices. In every moment we do have the choice. We can choose skillful thinking and action, or we can choose unskillful thinking and action. The Buddha points towards this lesson in his first teaching, The Four Noble Truths.

The Buddha was born Prince Siddhartha Gautama to a royal family living in the area we now call Nepal. He lived in the sixth century B.C. As a boy and young man, he led a protected and affluent lifestyle. But as he grew older, Prince Siddhartha wanted to see what life was like outside his father's kingdom and he left, at age 29, to explore the world and seek Enlightenment. For the first time in his life, he saw old people; he saw sick people; he saw a corpse. He realized that all human beings experience the same cycle of suffering: birth, illness, growing old, and dying. Because he wanted to relieve suffering for all sentient beings, he sought Enlightenment. After many years and after practicing many different techniques, he sat down and meditated under the Bodhi tree. It is there he attained Enlightenment and became the Buddha, the Enlightened One. His first teaching after his Enlightenment is "The Four Noble Truths."

The Four Noble Truths state that:

1. Life is suffering.

2. There is a cause for suffering.

3. Suffering can be overcome.

4. The way to overcome suffering is the eightfold path.

The life of an active alcoholic is definitely full of suffering. The cause of suffering, as the Buddha teaches us, is desire or craving. We want our pleasurable experiences to return or remain, and we want to quickly rid ourselves of unpleasant experiences. We are unable to accept the ebb and flow of life. When actively engaged in our addiction, we resist the reality of impermanence. This is what we learned in the first step. When we succumb to our craving for our addictive substance, we end up suffering in some fashion or another. We spend more money than we intended; we engage in behaviors and associate with people we wouldn't normally; we miss appointments; we lose jobs; we destroy relationships. You get the picture.

In The Third Noble Truth, we learn the good news from the Buddha that suffering can be overcome. We can be restored to a healthy, sane life by making our life choices based on Buddhist principles. At this point, I have touched briefly on only two items on The Eightfold Path: skillful thinking and skillful action. But this is enough for you to recognize that there is a way out of your suffering, a way out of your addiction.

The Buddha teaches that skillful thinking leads to happy thinking. Catch yourself having a happy thought. This takes patience in early recovery since there may not be an abundance of happy thoughts. But there are some! Pay attention. When you catch yourself having happy thoughts, stop and examine what is happening. What just happened? What are you doing? What is the happy thought? What does it feel like in your body? Are you smiling? Are you alone or with others? What time of day is it? Keep a daily journal of "happy thoughts" and your examination of them. Use this information to intentionally recreate happy thoughts in the future. You are learning to use awareness and intention to set a healthy direction for yourself.

The Buddha also teaches that unskillful thinking leads to unhappy results. Action that results from a mind under the influence of any of the three poisons is unskillful. Yikes! It seems we are poisoning ourselves with thoughts, not just with our addictive substance. It's time to find out about these other poisons. The three poisons are greed, hatred, and ignorance or delusion. Probably you are familiar with these poisons. We focused on the poison of delusion in Chapter One. Hatred and greed can lead to equally unhappy results. These poisons are not likely to disappear instantly. They have become habitual patterns of thought. Letting go of them involves shining awareness on them. By recognizing them, the habitual flow of thought is interrupted.

Be watchful for thoughts involving hatred and/or greed. When you notice you are having such a thought, simply pause. Take a deep breath in, clench your fists, and acknowledge the thought is there. Be aware of it. Then exhale, releasing the thought and relaxing your fingers. Now move on with your day. This pattern interrupt will only take a minute or two, but it will assist you in letting go of poisonous thoughts! Try it.

This second step along the recovery path is an exciting one! You are learning about your essential nature, your "Buddha Nature." Your "Buddha Nature" remains the same throughout your lifetime. You know you are accessing your "Buddha Nature" when you feel in sync with everything around you. Some call it being in "the zone." In the second step, you are also learning that your ego identity is non-essential. It shifts and morphs over the course of your life. The labels you used to describe yourself at age ten bear little resemblance to the labels you use today. In a very real way you are not the same person today that you were at age ten.

You are learning about different forms of mantra meditation and the benefits accrued from a meditation practice. In particular, you are learning to chant the "Odaimoku." And you are learning how to differentiate between skillful, sane thoughts and actions, and unskillful, insane thoughts and actions.

Morning Mantra Meditation, Chanting the Odaimoku

Prepare a space in your home for your morning meditation. By returning to the same space every day, you will automatically start to become calm, in anticipation of your meditation. You could use a small tabletop of some sort. Cover it with a clean cloth. Place a picture on the cloth. Choose a picture that helps you to become peaceful when you look at it. You could, perhaps, use a picture of trees, flowers, the ocean, or some other natural setting. You might want to light a candle and/or some incense.

Upon awakening, get out of bed and visit your bathroom to relieve yourself. After washing your hands, go directly to your meditation space and sit in front of the picture you chose. You can sit on a chair with your feet on the floor. You can sit on the floor using a meditation bench or cushion. Experiment with each position and find the one that is most comfortable for you.

Sit with your back straight. Place your hands together in gassho: palms together, wrists at your heart center, and fingers at a 45-degree angle from your body. Take a deep breath in and slowly let it out. This will help to center you. Make a small bow forward, keeping your back straight. Now begin chanting the Odaimoku – "Namu Myoho Renge Kyo." You can chant it as often as you like as long as you chant it at least three times. When you are finished chanting, make another small bow.

Congratulations! You are learning to make healthy choices and you are developing a meditation practice to grow your essential being, your "Buddha Nature." In Buddhism, the ordinary becomes extraordinary. Your recovery path can take you there as well. Enjoy the miracle of each sober moment.

Chapter Three

TAKING REFUGE

At this point in your journey into recovery, you open the gate of awareness and look at your life through a new lens. You remove the filters that shield you from the reality of your existence. You look clearly at what your life looks like under the influence of your addiction. Do you want to continue on with that life? Are the experiences you actually have when you are under the influence of your addictive substance the types of experiences you would choose for yourself? Would you wish these experiences on the people you love? Do you consider your addictive lifestyle one worthy of seeking?

Since stepping through the gate of awareness, you have been trying out a variety of new experiences. You experimented with relaxation techniques, with thought-stopping techniques, and with a variety of meditation and chanting techniques. You learned the story of Prince Siddhartha and his Enlightenment, becoming the

Buddha. You discovered and started to cultivate your own "Buddha Nature" within. Are these new experiences ones you find useful? Do they enhance your life? Are they ones you would wish to continue with and share with others?

It is time to make a decision. Do you want to continue with your addictive lifestyle? Or do you want to change your life in a way that would allow you to make better choices for yourself? You are not being asked to think about it; you are not being asked to get back to the question later; you are being asked to commit to a course of action now.

In traditional AA recovery programs, the course of action you are asked to commit to is that of turning your will and your life over to the care of "God as you understand Him." This was not something I was able to embrace on my recovery path. I had no personal understanding, or experience, of God. God is defined in the Oxford Canadian dictionary as "the creator and ruler of the universe" or "a superhuman being or spirit worshipped as having power over nature, human fortunes, etc." These definitions were meaningless to me. I was being asked to give my life up to the unknown in an act of faith. This made no sense to me whatsoever. I was told I could define God to be anything I wanted it to be and the suggestion was offered to me to consider God to simply stand for good and orderly direction. At that point, any purpose in using the term "God" became meaningless. If I can choose any meaning for a word, then that word no longer has any meaning.

My experience has led me to believe that the god that

others seek is really our true essence, our "Buddha Nature" which is within each of us. So, the decision you are being asked to make in this third step is about choosing to turn your will and your life over to the care of your "Buddha Nature." You are choosing the cultivation of your "Buddha Nature," your essential self, as opposed to choosing to continue with your addictive lifestyle. If you choose to curtail your addictive lifestyle and cultivate your "Buddha Nature," then you will be interested in knowing more about what that choice means.

You are choosing to turn away from your addictive lifestyle. This choice involves not drinking. The first two chapters provide you with many techniques to help you lessen cravings, avoid triggers, reach out to others, and generally make healthier choices in your life.

You are choosing to turn towards your "Buddha Nature" in order to live a happier, healthier, sane life. Your "Buddha Nature" is your essential self, your true nature, that place inside where you feel connected to all of life, where you are in the zone. It doesn't require thought. It simply is. Qualities of your essential self include peace, joy, interconnection, contentment, love, and true happiness. These qualities already exist within you. It is simply a question of accessing them.

Robert Holden, a happiness expert, reports in his video, "3 Happiness Myths Debunked," that 40% of what makes up long-term happiness are personal choices. This final step on the path of awareness is all about making a decision, a personal choice. Choose wellness! Make the decision to cultivate your "Buddha Nature." Allow your essential nature to grow. Allow happiness to permeate your life.

There are many different forms of Buddhism, but one common characteristic is that each "takes refuge" in the Buddha, the Dharma, and the Sangha. To take refuge means both to seek protection from harm and danger and also to seek spiritual guidance and direction. A Buddhist is a person who seeks protection and guidance by turning to the Buddha (the Enlightened One), the Dharma (the teachings of the Buddha), and the Sangha (the community that learns and practices the Buddha's teachings).

The Dharma includes all of the teachings of the Buddha. In Nichiren Shu Buddhism, the Lotus Sutra is considered to be the Buddha's supreme teaching. In order to take refuge in the dharma, you will need to read and study the Lotus Sutra. The recommended text in Nichiren Shu Buddhism is the one translated from the Chinese by Reverend Senchu Murano. It is available online at Amazon or from a Buddhist minister. If you cannot afford to purchase the book, there are other translations that are available online for free. It is important to study the Lotus Sutra under the guidance of a Nichiren Shu minister. Look online to see where the nearest Nichiren Shu Temple is and then contact the minister attached to that temple.

There are many beautiful stories and parables contained in the Lotus Sutra. The parable of the burning house helps to explain the need for diversity within Buddhism while establishing the Lotus Sutra as the supreme text. In this parable, there is a wealthy man who owns a very large house. The house has many rooms. All of his servants and all of his thirty children live in this house. One day when the wealthy man returns to his house, he sees that fires have broken out on all sides of his house. He runs down the hill to his house, shouting to his children to get out of the house. But the children are inside playing with their toys. They do not listen to their father, but instead continue playing with their toys while the house continues to burn.

The man realizes he must convince the children to leave the house or they will die. He tells them he has brought them special toys they want—three different kinds of carts—and that they can choose whichever one they want once they leave the house. The children all run outside and discover their father has brought only one type of cart. It is a magnificent cart, much more beautiful than any they had imagined. The wealthy man saves his children from the burning house and gives each of them one of the magnificent carts. The children are free from harm and happy.

In this parable, the wealthy man represents the Buddha. The children represent all human beings. The burning house represents the unexamined, unaware, unenlightened life. In order to save all human beings from the sufferings of this life (the first noble truth), the Buddha offers expedient teachings (the three different kinds of carts) to engage all humans no matter what their preoccupations are. The three different kinds of carts represent the various teachings of the Buddha. However, the one supreme teaching is the Lotus Sutra (the magnificent cart given to all of the children). It is by reading and studying the Lotus

Sutra that all humans are saved from suffering and become happy and content.

We take refuge in the Buddha. We take refuge in the Dharma, i.e. all of the Buddha's teachings but especially in his supreme teaching, the Lotus Sutra. And we take refuge in the Sangha, our spiritual community. This last refuge is especially important for the recovering addict because it marks the end of isolation and the breaking of silence. The Buddhist path is one taken with community. It is the same with the recovery path. We need connection and support from our fellow travelers. It is through this connection with others that we will learn about compassion, forgiveness, integrity, generosity, respect, gratitude, acceptance, and joy.

Alcoholics, when actively addicted, are suffering people. All suffering people can be helped if they seek refuge in the Buddha, the Dharma, and the Sangha. In Canada, addiction is now classified as an illness under the broad heading of "Mental Health and Addiction Services." Buddhism also views addiction as a sickness. For the addict, secrets become your illness. You need the support of a non-judging community. You need to share and connect with others in order to become healthy.

Once a decision is made, a commitment is made. Making a decision is a commitment that marks a turning point. You are turning away from your addictive lifestyle and turning towards your recovery lifestyle within Nichiren Shu Buddhism. It is not uncommon to formalize this turning point by taking a vow. A newly married couple makes a vow to one another during their wedding ceremony. The vow defines the turning point between being single and being married. If you wish to formalize your decision to give up alcohol and embrace Buddhism (your commitment in this third step along your recovery path), you may choose to take a vow as well.

If you live in a city where there is a Nichiren Shu Temple, then you could contact the minister there and arrange to talk about the possibility of a Taking Refuge ceremony. If you are not that fortunate, you can easily contact my minister, Rev. Kanjin Cederman through the temple website at enkyojibuddhistnetwork.org. Taking refuge is one of the first steps in becoming a Buddhist, in joining the Buddhist community.

Regardless of whether you participate in a Taking Refuge ceremony or not, it is important for you to create the habit of starting your day in front of your home altar. Up until this point, you have been starting your day by chanting "Namu Myoho Renge Kyo." Once you make this decision to leave your addictive life behind and embrace recovery with the assistance of Nichiren Shu Buddhism, you need to learn more about this spiritual path.

Each morning, Nichiren Shu Buddhists start the day in front of their home altar. A candle is lit to represent light or enlightenment. Incense is lit using the light from the candle. The burning of incense purifies the air and also represents purifying our senses. Thus the day begins by being reminded to keep one's senses clear, to not lay interpretation or judgment upon them. Being restored to sanity, becoming addiction-free, begins with seeing (or hearing, etc.) clearly. Start each day by chanting the Odaimoku in front of your simple home altar.

Whether you are chanting or meditating, you automatically become aware of your breath. The breath is the vehicle for unifying the body and the mind. In order to breathe as well as possible, it is helpful to learn how to clear the nasal passages. The procedure I was taught and have used for many years is to use a neti pot. It is a traditional Ayurvedic health practice.

A neti pot looks a bit like a teapot but has an elongated spout. They are available in most health stores. Fill your neti pot half full with warm distilled water, then mix in a saline solution, also available in most health stores. Lean over a sink, keep your chin down and in, and tilt your head to one side. Now place the spout of your neti pot in the upper nostril and pour the solution through one nostril and out the other. It takes a bit of practice so just experiment till it is working for you. I find keeping the chin down to be the most helpful tip. Allow the solution to run freely from one nostril to the other for a minute or so. Then clear the nostrils using a tissue. Tilt your head to the other side and repeat the procedure. With clear nasal passages you will breathe more easily and reduce headaches caused by sinus congestion and allergies.

There are a number of controlled breathing practices that can be helpful in early recovery. The one I find most useful is alternate nostril breathing. It is easy to do, does not take much time, and helps bring balance to the mind. It calms the mind so is very effective when experiencing racing thoughts that dominate in anxiety or when craving. It is also an excellent practice to engage in prior to meditation.

Place the index finger and middle finger on the bridge of your nose. Close your eyes. Using your thumb to gently block your right nostril, breathe in through your left nostril to the count of 4. Block your left nostril using your ring finger and hold your breath to the count of 4. Now lift your thumb and exhale through your right nostril to the count of 4. Keeping your ring finger on your left nostril, breathe in through your right nostril to the count of 4. Close your right nostril with your thumb and hold your breath for the count of 4. Release your ring finger and breathe out through your left nostril to the count of 4. Keeping your thumb on your right nostril, breathe in through your left nostril to the count of 4. Repeat this sequence as often as you like being sure to end on the out breath through the left nostril.

In early recovery, one or two minutes will suffice. As you become more comfortable with this practice, you can increase the count from 4 to 5 to 6, and you can extend your practice to three minutes, then four minutes. You will discover what time frames work best for you in different situations.

Awareness of the breath is critical in connecting mind and body. Another practice that uses the breath specifically for this purpose is yoga. I highly recommend you try yoga. It will help you improve strength, flexibility, and balance while using your breath to help you stay focused on the present moment. Join a yoga class. You will receive instruction and guidance, and you will be in the company of like-minded individuals.

You are accomplishing many things while in the field

of awareness. Be sure to stay here long enough to feel confident that you are seeing the world "as it is." If you are keeping a journal, you can use it to check back and confirm that what you think happened is or is not what actually happened. Sometimes another person can serve as a mirror as well, reflecting back to you what they saw happening.

The primary job while in the field of awareness is to lift the veil of delusion. It is likely that some kind of traumatic event initiated this procedure. Perhaps your partner asked you to leave. Perhaps you were charged with driving under the influence and/or spent the night in jail. Or perhaps, like me, you tried to quit drinking and failed. Something brought you to pick up this book and look for an answer. There is an answer in the pages of this book.

You are more aware of what craving a drink feels like in your body and in your mind. You are aware of some triggers (HALT) that can set up craving. You tried out a variety of techniques to interrupt and stop craving. Perhaps you got help from your medical doctor. Perhaps you completed a treatment program. The end result is the same. You now have experienced at least a short period of continuous sobriety. Whatever your benchmark was, you achieved it! For me it was two weeks. Once I could remain sober for more than two weeks, I knew that what I was doing was getting me what I wanted. It's not unusual to relapse occasionally in early recovery. It is part of the process for some recovering alcoholics. Just start again. You will reach your goal as long as you keep trying.

While you are working towards your sobriety goal, you start to learn how to live a healthier life by cultivating your "Buddha Nature." You commit to your sobriety and your Buddhist lifestyle each morning in front of your home altar. You chant "Namu Myoho Renge Kyo" every day. You talk with the Nichiren Shu minister in the temple in your city, or contact a minister online through seattlebuddhist.org. You read and study the Lotus Sutra with the guidance of a minister.

You begin to form a recovery support network. You can't do recovery from alcohol addiction alone. Your recovery network will include your minister and possibly other members of your sangha. It might include your doctor or an addiction counselor if you have one. It might include an aftercare group if you chose treatment. Invite into your recovery circle those people who are supporting your new way of life.

Affirmations Meditation

Affirmations have a powerful influence on our lives, but are the most beneficial when our mind is relaxed and receptive. Therefore we will start with a mantra-based silent meditation prior to repeating our affirmations.

Sit in a comfortable position with your back straight. Close your eyes. Place your hands in your lap with your left hand resting on your right palm. Touch your thumbs together to form a circle. Take a deep breath in filling your chest and your belly. Hold it for the count of 3, and release your breath through your nose. Take another deep breath in and repeat the procedure. Now allow your breathing to return to normal, not controlling it in any way. As you breathe in, repeat the sound "So" silently. As you breathe out, repeat the sound "Hum." Continue matching the So-Hum mantra to your breath for about five minutes. Don't worry about the exact time. When you have lost your sense of time and are feeling relaxed, you can start silently repeating the following affirmations:

May I remain sober.

May I see my world as it is.

May I make healthy choices.

Say all three affirmations in order, and then repeat them. Return to the So-Hum meditation for one or two minutes before opening your eyes.

You are in the field of Awareness. When you feel comfortable here and are committed to your decision to turn towards your "Buddha Nature" in order to improve your life, then you are ready to walk through the next gate. When you pass through the next gate, the gate of Introspection, you will learn to face your secrets and release them. It sounds daunting. It sounds scary. But you can do it. Hold my hand. Let's go!

THE SECOND GATE
INTROSPECTION

REPENTANCE

A tiny needle sinks into water. Rain falls – it cannot float in the air. These are natural laws. A person who kills a tiny ant falls into hell. Thus, a person who kills a human being falls into hell.

However, a huge rock can float on water if it is placed on a ship. A raging fire can be extinguished by the power of water. Without repentance, even a small sin can make a man fall into hell. On the other hand, with sincere repentance, even great sins can be erased.

(Nichiren's writings, March, 1276, 54 years old, at Minobu, *Showa Teihon*, p.1158)

Chapter Four

THE PRECEPTS

It is time to take an honest look at your life from a moral perspective. In the traditional AA program, this would encompass steps four and five. You are asked to make a searching and fearless moral inventory of yourself, and then to admit to God, to yourself, and to another human being the exact nature of your wrongs. I completed a few moral inventories over the first ten years or so of my sobriety. For me, it was like peeling an onion in that each layer came off in its own time. Clearly I did not admit anything to God, since there was no God in my life. However, there was definitely a benefit from taking responsibility for my own actions and sharing this with a trusted individual.

When Bill W co-founded the AA program, he was a defeated alcoholic who had been hospitalized many times and everyone had given up any hope of him gaining sobriety. He was told by a friend, a former drinking buddy, that the only hope for him was to admit complete defeat and turn his life over to the care of God. As it turns out, Bill W did have a profound spiritual experience shortly after his friend's visit. He never drank again and shared his experience with others through the AA program. There is no doubt that the AA program has helped many alcoholics and addicts lead a healthier life. It is also true that very few people experience such a profound spiritual conversion as that which Bill W did. I did not experience one. No one I know in the AA program experienced one.

On the recovery path presented in this book, you will be asked to take steps that are accessible to everyone and that, if followed, you will learn principles and practices that will enhance your life. You will begin to see clearly how some of your choices have led to harm – for yourself and for others around you. And you will learn how to replace those choices and habits with healthier choices and create new habits.

Our first question is how to approach a moral inventory. There are two main branches of Buddhism: Theravada Buddhism and Mahayana Buddhism. Nichiren Shu Buddhism falls within the branch of Mahayana Buddhism. All Mahayana Buddhists follow a moral code identified as the five precepts. A Mahayana Buddhist will strive to abstain from 1) killing any living being, 2) taking what is not given, 3) indulging in harmful sexual behavior, 4) false speech, and 5) taking intoxicants.

In Buddhism, there is no guilt. The goal is to learn from our own mistakes and from mistakes of others. We reflect on these moral precepts, not to uncover our "bad" behavior, but rather to learn a better way to approach similar situations in the future. We will learn to see our life through sober eyes, to remove the dust from the mirror.

To live your life without killing any living being is almost impossible. These precepts are standards to strive towards, not necessarily to achieve with perfection. In order to strive towards these precepts, you will need to bring awareness and mindfulness to your actions. Your inventory will be a written inventory. Get a pad of paper and write down the heading "Not to Kill." Spend some time contemplating how you would define a living being. Talk with your Buddhist minister and study some of the Buddhist literature. Learning and studying are critical in Buddhism. For the purposes of this book, we will use the following definition: a living being is a being that has both breath and consciousness.

Think back over your life and try to recall times when you killed living beings. This would include killing insects and killing animals while hunting or fishing. Perhaps you have killed pests or even pets. Perhaps you have killed a human being while driving under the influence of drugs or alcohol. Bring all of these situations to mind and write them down. Make a list. Without an awareness of what you have done and an admission of who/what you have killed, you will carry the karma for that action. We will come back to the list later, but for now, simply make the list and then put it aside.

Get out a fresh piece of paper and write the heading "Not to Steal." What does the phrase "to abstain from taking what is not given" mean to you? It might include stealing articles from a store or someone's home. It might include stealing money from a bank, or a cash register, or someone's wallet. It might include stealing alcohol or drugs. It might include stealing intellectual property from a boss or co-worker. Again, it is important for you to sort out for yourself what this concept means to you. Study your Buddhist books and talk to your Buddhist minister. Be guided by what you learn. Then make a list of every time you can recall taking something that was not freely given. When you think you are done, put the paper aside for later.

The next precept heading is "Not to Indulge in Harmful Sexual Behavior." Write it at the top of your next page. Again, talk to your Buddhist minister and read your Buddhist books. Determine what harmful sexual behavior means to you. Remember that within the context of the precepts, harmful includes harm to self and/or harm to others. Perhaps you had a secret affair outside the bonds of marriage. Perhaps you had a sexual encounter without consent. Perhaps you knowingly passed on a sexually transmitted disease. Perhaps you misled someone solely for sexual purposes. If deceit or force were involved, then it harmed someone. If it was a secretive sexual encounter or experience, then it hurt someone. If it was against the law, then it hurt someone. Healthy sexuality always involves a balance of power. Both people need to be in an even balance of power. If you used your position as a boss or leader to influence someone to engage in sexual activities with you, then you hurt someone. Be thorough.

Remember that secrets are at the core of your illness, your addiction.

Our examination of the fourth precept will fall under the heading, "Not to Lie." Again, write that heading at the top of your page. Do your study, and learn from your Buddhist minister. What is a lie? Is it okay to be silent when you know others are operating on misinformation? Is it a lie if you believed it to be true at the time you said it? What is false speech? What if you discover that something you said was untrue? Is it your responsibility to let people know? Where does gossip fit in? Is it okay to pass on gossip at any time, let alone without checking the facts first? Be sure you have a clear understanding of what it means to abstain from false speech. Then make your list.

The final precept is the clearest for an addict. Write the heading, "To Abstain from Taking Intoxicants." When did you take your first drink? Write out your drinking/using history. What did you drink? How much did you drink? How often? If you have been to a treatment center, then you likely completed a drinking/using history there. Because you are addicted to alcohol (and possibly drugs, and/or specific behaviors), there is no questioning that your usage caused you and others harm. That is the premise of this book, and the purpose of every exercise is to teach you how to stop hurting yourself and others.

In Buddhism, we seek the middle way. In reality, in our human life, the middle way is flexible. It is not a defined place. We seek fluidity, not static truth. There is a need to overcome the dualism of good/bad, right/wrong, etc. In your recovery you will seek and find the path that leads to self-knowledge. But this "place" will shift as your life circumstances shift. Your "place" of balance will not be the same "place" as someone else's. Each of us is responsible for our own life and the choices we make.

When your lists are complete, take a deep breath. This is hard work. Don't overexert yourself. You do not need to complete all five lists in one sitting. My suggestion is that you spend your first session reading Buddhist books and contemplating the meaning for you of each of the key concepts in each of the five precepts. Then book an appointment with your Buddhist minister and discuss your ideas with him or her. Be open to hearing new ideas. Only then, start your lists. Maybe complete one list per session. Maybe complete them all at one time. You will know when you get started what feels right for you. Trust yourself.

When all five lists are completed, go back over each item and discover what you were feeling when it occurred and what basic need it filled in your life. In order to do that, a quick overview of feelings and needs as taught by Marshall Rosenberg in his book, *Nonviolent Communication*, will be helpful.

Rachelle Lamb was my first NVC teacher. At that very first exposure to Nonviolent Communication, sometimes known as a Language of Compassion or a Language of Life, I received a booklet Rachelle wrote. It is called *Essentials of Nonviolent Communication*. In it, she describes the needs that all human beings share. These include needs for autonomy (choice, independence, space), needs for connection (acceptance, closeness, inclusion, safety, trust), needs for harmony (beauty, ease, order, peace), needs for honesty (clarity, integrity, self-expression), needs for meaning (celebration, contribution, growth, participation), needs for play (joy, humor, stimulation), and needs for physical wellbeing (air, food, rest, shelter, safety, touch).

When these needs are met, you might feel confident, connected, engaged, excited, exhilarated, grateful, hopeful, inspired, joyful, peaceful, or refreshed. When these needs are not being met, you might feel afraid, annoyed, confused, disconnected, embarrassed, fatigued, pained, sad, tense, or vulnerable. When I was in early recovery, I was aware of only three feelings: mad, sad, or glad. There is so much more to experience in this life! Start by identifying your different feelings over the course of a day. Use the feelings list here or expand it by looking up more extensive lists online under "nonviolent communication."

One exercise I found useful, and I still use it today when I'm overwhelmed or confused, is to make a deck of "feelings" cards and a deck of "needs" cards. These can be purchased online at www.nvcproducts.com. They are called "Grok" and consist of the two decks of cards and instructions for a number of interactive games. For the purposes I am going to describe, it is easy to make your own cards. Cut out small pieces of paper or Bristol board and write one feeling word on each piece to create your feelings deck. Then write one needs word on individual pieces as well for your needs deck.

When you want to explore your feelings, get your

decks of cards and find a quiet space where you will not be disturbed. Take out your feelings deck. One at a time, place a feelings word in front of you. Ask yourself, "Is this what I'm feeling right now?" Accept your first, automatic response. If the answer is yes, place the card in your yes pile. If the answer is no, place the card in your no pile. Do not go back and change any of your answers. When you have divided up all of your feelings cards, gather up the no pile and put it away.

Now take your pile of yes cards and spread them out on a table, or on the floor, anywhere that you can see all of them at once. Say each of the words aloud several times. Notice how your body feels when you say each word. Do some words elicit a stronger reaction than others? Are you clenching your jaw or making a fist? Does your voice falter when you say some words? Are you crying or screaming? Pay attention to how your emotional feelings live in your body.

After you have repeated each feelings word a few times, you may notice that your reactions are not as intense. The feelings word loses its strength as a sensation in your body and becomes an idea or thought in your mind. Notice that strong emotions do not last. All emotions, all sensations, all thoughts simply pass through. This is impermanence. With practice, we are able to observe them as they pass through our mind.

Looking at your group of feelings words, ask yourself the question, "What did I want when I felt this way?" Pick up your needs card deck and turn over each card, one at a time. For each card, ask if it fits for your situation. For example you might ask, "Was I looking for love?" or "Was I looking for security?" or "Was I looking for fun and play?" Place each card in the yes pile or the no pile. Again, put the no pile away and lay out the cards in your yes pile so you can see them all. These are the beautiful needs you are seeking right now. They are life serving.

We sometimes use harmful means to try to achieve our goals, our needs. That doesn't mean there is anything wrong with the need. But we do have to learn other ways to fulfil our needs in ways that do not harm ourselves or harm others. These feelings and needs cards can broaden your repertoire of feelings and needs. Awareness is the first step in changing behavior.

Once you are familiar with a wider range of feelings and needs words as they apply to you, you are ready to go back to your five lists from your precepts headings. For each item on your list, ask yourself, "What was I feeling when this happened?" Write it down. Then ask yourself, "What need was I trying to meet?" or "What was the need behind the feeling?"

Look for patterns. Try to see the beautiful need behind the behavior. Your moral inventory is now complete and you are ready to share it with another person. Choosing the right person can be difficult.

It is interesting to notice that within the NVC community there has been a transition away from the title "Nonviolent Communication" and towards the acceptance of "Compassionate Communication" or "A Language of Compassion." I see the same type of movement within recovery communities and treatment centers. However, there is a huge difference in the two as well. In the NVC community, it is a transition based on word choice only. The NVC community has always been based in compassion, even when its name did not reflect that.

In the recovery community, it is a transition based on practice. When the *Big Book of Alcoholics Anonymous* was written, the alcoholics it was directed at were those similar to Bill W, i.e. those whom everyone had given up on. It was believed an alcoholic had to "bottom out" before being able to get well. Part of the "bottoming out" procedure occurred as a result of steps four and five. An alcoholic needed to declare complete defeat, focus on and admit that he or she was worthless in order to be emptied out and rebuild a new life. This procedure was adopted by a number of treatment centers. Although the procedure was most likely adopted with good intentions, many alcoholics were broken during this process and never recovered. Some committed suicide.

Acting with sympathy without understanding can lead to harmful actions. Most treatment centers I am aware of are no longer using these methods. In the 1990s, I trained in three separate treatment centers in order to work as a teacher-counselor in a school-based aftercare program. Two were in the United States (Heartview Foundation in Mandan, North Dakota, and Rimrock Foundation in Billings, Montana). The third, Whitespruce, was a residential adolescent treatment center in Yorkton, Saskatchewan. It was evident at that time that the model was beginning to shift. Over the past ten years I have watched a person close to me go through two different treatment centers in Canada. It is clear that the treatment model used today is much more holistic in nature. However, there is still an over-reliance on the twelve steps of Alcoholics Anonymous.

In Buddhist ethics, compassion is the dominant determinant in one's actions. Compassion needs to be balanced with wisdom. By asking the questions about your feelings and needs when reviewing your five lists from your precepts review, you started to develop compassion for yourself. In a similar fashion, you will want to look for an individual who displays compassion as a dominant characteristic when deciding with whom you will share your precepts lists. This person will display wisdom as well. Do not be fooled by a person displaying intellectual wisdom. This is not the type of wisdom required in the person you are seeking. Look for a person who is able to see humans as they are.

If you were fortunate enough to discuss the precepts with a Nichiren Shu Buddhist minister, then this is the person you will want to share your results with. If that is not possible, perhaps you will be able to find a Buddhist minister in another of the Mahayana schools of Buddhism. Another great place to look is within the NVC community. You can go online and find trained people in most cities in North America. These people are trained in Compassionate Communication. They have practiced and understand the importance of "holding space" for someone as an act of empathy.

Loving Kindness Meditation

It is very important when making your moral inventory that you do not allow yourself to become despondent over things you have done in your past. This meditation will help you to accept and love yourself as you go through this difficult assignment. The ultimate goal will be to release your past and move forward in your life committed to a new set of principles. These principles or precepts will help you to take a stance or hold a position.

Usually a loving kindness meditation is directed to self, and then it is directed to others. At this point in your recovery, we will limit the loving kindness meditation to only you.

Sit comfortably with your back straight to allow the free flow of air and energy. Close your eyes. Place your hands on your thighs, palms up to indicate your willingness to receive. Take a few deep breaths in and out. Allow your breathing to return to normal, not controlling it in any way. Bring your attention to the area of your heart. Now, visualize an image of yourself as a child. Repeat the following statements while maintaining the clear image of you as a child:

May I be safe and free from all harm.

May I be well in body and in mind.

May I be happy.

May I be peaceful and at ease.

Repeat these statements several times. Then, sit in silence with eyes closed and release the image of yourself as a child. Sit in silence for another minute or two, allowing everything you have said to yourself to sink in. When you are ready, open your eyes.

Facing yourself honestly and accepting your role in harm that was caused to yourself and others is one of the hardest exercises for an alcoholic. We lived our addicted lives behind the veil of delusion, lying to ourselves as well as others. Ironically, it is this newly found honesty that brings forth freedom.

Chapter Five

PLANTING THE ROOTS OF VIRTUE

In the traditional twelve steps as laid out in Alcoholics Anonymous, steps six and seven deal with identifying your defects of character, becoming ready to have them removed, and having God remove them. The problem I experienced with this approach is the negative focus on defects and the sense of emptiness upon removal. There is no suggestion as to how to build positive behaviors. I find it much easier to change behavior by replacing old behavior that is no longer working with new behavior that has a better chance of meeting my needs.

When we completed our moral inventory in Chapter Four, we discovered the needs that were behind the behaviors we chose and we discovered that those behaviors were not working for us. We need a new set of behaviors to try out. If we replace old behaviors with new behaviors, then the old behaviors will naturally lessen and be eradicated. At the same time, we gradually build new behaviors and discover what truly works for us. We plant the seeds of our new behaviors in the mud of our addicted lives. From this seed, we discover and nourish new behaviors that blossom into joyful living. Just as the beautiful lotus flower is planted in mud, our sober, healthy, joyful lives are planted in the mud of our addictions. Like the lotus, you have to be in the mud. Both are necessary.

Active alcoholics are not bad people. They are misguided people who make poor choices and consequently do not recognize their true value. There is a parable in the Lotus Sutra that helps teach this distinction. It is called the parable of the poor son.

The son runs away from his father's home when he is a young boy. He travels to many different places, never staying in one area for very long. He works as a hired hand doing menial work for a short period of time and then moves on. He doesn't put down roots. He doesn't form lasting relationships with anyone. He doesn't acquire any personal belongings.

When the son leaves his father's house, the father is very upset. He worries about the wellbeing of his son and searches for him in many places but never finds him. Eventually the father gives up his search and establishes a new home in a new place. He is very wealthy and employs many servants. His house is like a king's palace and he has storerooms full of jewels and other treasures.

After many years of wandering, the son happens upon the place where his father has settled. He stands outside his father's estate and peers inside. He doesn't know this is his own father's home. Seeing the magnificence of the grounds and the house, he decides it is too elegant for a lowly worker such as himself. He is covered in dirt and wears ragged clothing. He turns away in search of what he believes would be a better fit for him.

The father sees the dirty wanderer and, even though many years have passed, he recognizes him as his long lost son. The father sends some of his servants after the son to bring him back. Unfortunately, the son did not see or recognize his father. He believes the servants are going to harm him and he is filled with fear and tries to escape from the servants. The father is watching this unfold and calls off his servants.

The father understands that if he wants his son to come to his estate he must approach his son from the same level as his son occupies at that time. Although the son is the rightful heir to all of the estate and all of his father's riches, he does not know this. He sees himself as a lowly wanderer. The father understands this and sets about to teach his son who he really is. This time the servants are dressed in rags when they approach the son. They offer him lowly work, clearing dirt. But they offer him twice the usual pay, and in this way, the son is brought onto his father's estate. Occasionally the father dresses in simple clothes and encourages his son in his work.

Many more years pass, and slowly the son is given more responsibility. Eventually he becomes the manager of the entire estate. In spite of this, he continues to view himself as "less than." Eventually his self-confidence grows. By this time the father is very old and near death. The father calls his son and other important people to his bedside and tells everyone gathered that the manager is indeed his son and that he will inherit all of the wealthy man's possessions. The son is able to accept that he is the wealthy man's son and celebrate his identity.

There are many teachings in this parable. The first is that it is the son who runs away from his father's home. The father did not send him away. In the parable the wealthy father is the Buddha. The son represents each of us. As active alcoholics, we leave the Buddha's home and run away. Like the wandering vagabond son, an alcoholic's world becomes one full of suffering, loss of connection, fear of others, and diminished self-worth. The active alcoholic loses sight of his/her own worth. The connection to his "Buddha Nature" is lost.

The first job the wealthy father gives his son is clearing away dirt. In a similar fashion, the first job on the recovery path is one of clearing away dirt. You need to be able to see the dirt in order to clean it up. The Gate of Awareness allows you to see clearly where the dirt in your life is. The Gate of Introspection allows you to clear away the dirt of your alcoholic life. This is the purpose of your moral inventory.

Once you look at your completed moral inventory, it is easy to see what choices and behaviors led to suffering for you or others. Now is the time to clear away the dirt of your alcoholic living, to let go of old patterns of behavior. The father stayed close to his son during this phase of rebuilding and offered a great deal of encouragement. Seek out people who are able to support and encourage you in your new way of life. Be sure to connect with your "Buddha Nature" every day through chanting and meditation.

Remember that it took a long time for the son to move from feelings of inferiority to feelings of competence and worth. There is much work to do. It is a process, not an instant fix. But it is a process that will lead you to freedom and joy.

So what is this process? What is the next job after clearing away the dirt? The father gave his son new jobs in order to allow the son to acquire competence and self-worth. In a similar fashion, the recovering alcoholic needs to try out new behaviors. It is not enough to discover what didn't work. Now, you need to find out what does work by trying on new behaviors.

The new behaviors that Mahayana Buddhists strive for are called The Six Perfections or Paramitas. Notice that these are behaviors to strive for. They are goals or standards against which each of us can examine our behavior in order to make informed, experience-based decisions about our choices as we move through this human life. Remember that in the parable, it takes the son many years to learn new skills and even more years to acquire self-confidence and self-worth. This may be true for you as well. Do not expect perfection. Bill W says in the book *Alcoholics Anonymous*, "We claim spiritual progress, not spiritual perfection" (p.60). You do not fail if you are not perfect. You are not a bad person if you are not perfect. You are a human being trying your best to live a healthy, peaceful life. You are a recovering alcoholic trying to learn to live without your addiction.

You cannot learn without making mistakes, but you need to bring the light of awareness to your actions. The Buddha's path is grounded in common sense and in careful observation of reality. Your worst experiences have become your greatest treasures. Your worst experiences are identified when you complete your moral inventory. Now they become your greatest treasure. How? They identify what is not working in your life and spur you on to seek change. It is not the case that your actions when actively addicted were "bad" or "evil." There is no fight between good and evil in Buddhism. Both are needed. It is thanks to your addictive behaviors that you are seeking a better life now. The beautiful and undefiled lotus flower blooms in a muddy swamp.

The first of the Six Perfections is Dana. Dana can be translated as giving or generosity. By developing an attitude of generosity, you will be able to let go of greed and self-centeredness. Dana implies a sincere desire to help others. If you have an expectation of recognition or reward, then you are not practicing Dana. There can be no selfishness attached to your giving. To practice Dana is to learn to give freely.

I find this much more difficult than it appears at first glance. Remember that we are now in the Garden of Introspection. It is important to look inside and discover our intentions and expectations. If you are logging volunteer hours in order to fulfill a requirement in a social work program you are taking, then your volunteer hours are not truly Dana. You are benefitting from the volunteer effort and perhaps would not be doing it otherwise. It is a training experience on the path to Dana but not Dana itself. However, it is a starting place.

If you are not experienced in giving, you will need to learn the skill. Only after the practice of giving becomes automatic will you be able to work on your intention and expectations. We will start with the practice of giving. There are several ways to give to others. One way is to give property. When we introduced needs in our personal inventory, we did not discuss a hierarchy of needs. But there are some basic needs that must be met before anyone can realistically move towards higher needs. Basic physical survival needs that all human beings share include our need for food, air, water, shelter, safety, rest/sleep, exercise, health, and touch.

Because these are basic needs that all humans share but not all human beings experience, this is an easy place to discover the act of giving property. You could give food to your local food bank. You could give blankets, toiletries, and clothing to a homeless shelter. You could give money for health-related research.

Another way of giving is to give your time. Keeping the focus on basic human needs, you could volunteer time working at your local soup kitchen preparing food and serving it to those in need. You could volunteer your time at a local hospital holding babies. You could volunteer your time at a nursing home teaching a yoga class. You could volunteer at a school reading to/with young reluctant readers. You could volunteer to canvass for funds for health-related research such as diabetes, Alzheimer's and other dementias, heart and stroke, etc.

Another way of giving is through active love. A great way to start this practice is to give a smile to a stranger. You could give a genuine compliment to at least one person every day. You could offer to help with immigrants and refugees, or other marginalized populations.

Once you begin to practice giving, you will notice that it feels good to give and to help others; however, this is not the lesson to be learned. It is an important step along the way. It teaches awareness of inner feelings. Knowing this will help you choose healthier activities when you notice you are experiencing feelings of disconnect or discomfort. Rather than isolating yourself and ruminating on your disconnect, you can choose to give to others. You will feel better. At this level, you are still learning.

After much practice of freely giving, you will eventually notice that your intention in giving is simply to help others and your expectation does not involve reward or recognition for yourself. This is the practice of Dana.

The second of the Six Perfections is Sila. Sila means virtue, morality, discipline, or proper conduct. Sila is achieved by practicing the Five Precepts. We became familiar with the Five Precepts by looking at our past actions and compiling a moral inventory. Now we use the same moral guide, the Five Precepts, to help us make healthy choices in each moment going forward.

A moral code is about how to behave. It is about our actions, including our speech. It requires both discipline and awareness to implement. You learned many techniques in the Garden of Awareness that are easily transferrable to choices you will make in the moral sphere. The same techniques you learned and practiced in order to deal with cravings in early recovery will now assist you in practicing Sila. Just as you learned to recognize what thoughts, feelings, and body sensations accompany cravings, you can learn and become aware of what thoughts, feelings, and body sensations accompany other reactive, harmful behaviors.

Review the Five Precepts on a regular basis – once a day, or once a week. Ask your Buddhist minister for methods to do this. Experiment and see what works for you. Ask yourself if you have killed any living being. Did you take anything that wasn't freely given? Did you engage in any harmful sexual behavior? Did you speak false information? Did you consume intoxicants? Journal about these episodes to determine what was going on in your thoughts, your feelings and your bodily sensations prior to any of these events. Then look at the outcome. What happened after you participated in the activity?

By shining the light of introspection on your actions, you will begin to see more clearly what leads you to make the choices you do, and to interrupt that chain of events in order to change your choices in the future if that is your wish. Gradually you will learn how to examine your life – your thoughts, feelings, body sensations, actions, and outcomes. The secret to a healthy, happy life is to understand that the quality of your life is determined by the choices you make. Without introspection, you are not making choices. You are simply reacting.

When you commit to living your life in accordance

with a moral code, you commit to a disciplined life. Examining your life choices requires discipline. Ironically, it is this same discipline that leads to freedom – freedom from cravings and the drama and trauma of an active alcoholic lifestyle, as well as freedom from reactivity and the negative consequences of thoughtless actions.

The third Perfection is Ksanti, which translates as patience. Other descriptors that may help with your understanding of Ksanti are tolerance, acceptance, composure, and endurance. One dimension of patience is the ability to endure or withstand some form of personal hardship or difficulty. This hardship may come in the form of a natural disaster, the loss of a loved one, being fired from your job, experiencing chronic pain, failing an exam. The hardship may be big or relatively small. The question is simply how do you handle yourself when confronted with loss, with pain, with disappointment? Do you stuff your feelings and get stuck? Alternatively, are you consumed by your feelings and become lost? Or are you able to endure? Are you able to allow yourself to fully feel and then move into acceptance?

Another dimension or aspect of patience is the ability to have patience with other people. The need for a general practice of having patience with others is most notable in a setting where we spend a great deal of time with others on a regular basis. This could be your family home, your rooming house, your work place, or any similar gathering place. In any setting where people gather there will be personality differences. How do you handle yourself when someone holds an opposing point of view from your own? How do you handle it when one person dominates a conversation? How do you handle it when someone interrupts you? When someone forgets an important piece of information you shared with him/her? When someone requires extra time to complete a simple task? These are all examples of situations requiring simple patience, tolerance, and acceptance. I'm sure you can think of many more based on your own experience.

In the previous examples, it is possible to become impatient with someone simply because he/she is unintentionally annoying you. Perhaps you are in a hurry to get somewhere but your mother can't find her purse and her search for it is going to make you late. Patience is required. You can tell yourself she needs help and join in the search. She isn't deliberately trying to make you late. Perhaps she is becoming forgetful and misplacing items regularly. Because you are able to identify the difficulty the other person is having, it becomes easier to accept the situation and practice patience.

The more difficult situation when practicing patience with others is when you know or discover that someone has deliberately harmed you. It is far more difficult to have tolerance for another's behavior when the person intended harm towards you. But it is still important to practice Ksanti in these circumstances, perhaps especially in these circumstances. The harm may come verbally – in the form of lies and gossip with the intention of character assassination or bringing into question your abilities. The harm may come physically – the other person assaults you in some fashion. In these situations it is often wise to seek professional assistance to help you determine appropriate boundaries and assess whether you want to press legal charges.

You may decide to terminate the relationship. You may decide to give the person another chance. Every situation is unique. There is no one-answer-fits-all. However, no matter what the practical outcome of the event is, your moral outcome is to practice tolerance. In situations of this nature that I have dealt with, I have sometimes terminated the relationship; I have sometimes placed clear boundaries on the relationship, and I have sometimes given the person another chance. In every situation, I sought spiritual guidance regarding how to best let go of the pain I felt.

One piece of advice I received and practice is to pray for the other person. This does not mean I need to keep him/her in my life. I can decide to exclude someone from my life but, at the same time, pray that he/she finds peace and happiness in life. This method has worked in this type of situation every time I used it! Sometimes I prayed for the other person every day for a week, sometimes for a month, and occasionally it has been longer. But it works every time if I keep at it. It allows me to protect myself while still practicing tolerance. It releases the pain and allows me to move forward with my life again.

Another piece of advice I have used is to release pain through a ritual. Often pain lies just beneath anger. Anger can be the end result of a painful memory. It is one of the most dangerous and toxic emotions. If you are angry with someone for the pain they caused you, then the first step in releasing that pain is to acknowledge that it is present in you. There is no point in pretending it isn't there. Journal about all the reasons you are upset with this person. Then look at the situation from an observer's point of view. Pretend you are watching the scene unfold on a movie screen. Ask yourself who your angry feelings are helping. Who are they hurting? One of my sponsors in the AA program once said to me, "You have been hurt enough in your life. Now you are only hurting yourself more by reliving these experiences." Until that moment, I didn't realize I was the one causing my pain.

The ritual I use is a fire ritual. I write a letter to the person saying everything I would like to say to them directly, and then I release the person, the situation, and the feelings attached to it by burning the letter. On some occasions I have burned objects I own that I see as being attached to the situation or person. This has been an extremely liberating process for me. I encourage you to try it.

The fourth Perfection is Virya Paramita. Virya can be translated as energy, diligence, or effort. Practicing the recovery path on a daily basis requires effort. Practicing the Buddhist path on a daily basis requires effort. Without effort there is no recovery from addiction. Without effort there is no Buddhist path. It is with effort that practice becomes habitual and energy is released. With this energy, you are able to live life to the fullest.

The fifth Perfection is Dhyana Paramita. This is all about meditation, focus, concentration, and contemplation. The goal is to abide in our "Buddha Nature," our true essence.

From this place we are able to see life "as it is." All forms of meditation are helpful in accessing our "Buddha Nature." There will be a more in-depth discussion of meditation in Chapter Eight.

The last of the six Perfections is Prajna Paramita. Prajna refers to wisdom or insight. This is a natural result of a daily meditation practice. I became a certified meditation teacher after training at The Chopra Center in Carlsbad, California. Deepak Chopra teaches that there are seven states of consciousness. The first three can be classified as mundane in that they refer to states of consciousness that can be accessed in this everyday world. The first is deep sleep. The second is dreaming, and the third is our waking state. In our waking state we access our world and interpret our world through our sense organs. We perceive the world to contain solids, gasses, and fluids. We perceive time to be linear. For the most part, we conduct ourselves as if this waking consciousness were all there is to life.

Deepak Chopra teaches that there are four higher levels of consciousness that can be accessed through meditation. These higher levels of consciousness can be classified as supra mundane in that they are developed through the realization of the truth of the reality of all things. Deepak Chopra's names for these higher levels of consciousness are Transcendence Consciousness, Cosmic Consciousness, Divine Consciousness, and Unified Consciousness. The highest level of consciousness, Unified Consciousness, is the wisdom that is taught in Chapter 2 of *The Lotus Sutra*. In Chapter 2 of *The Lotus Sutra*, the Buddha is talking to his disciple, Sariputra. The Buddha tells Sariputra that he, the

Buddha, has been using expedients to teach the dharma, but that the truth is there is only one Buddha-vehicle. The highest truth, the highest teaching is the knowledge of the equality and differences of all things.

The wisdom teaching is that all phenomena are without self-essence or independent existence. In the true reality, there is no subject-object separation at all. We are all one. All beings, all objects, all events are interconnected.

Meditation for Letting Go

While we are in the Garden of Introspection, we spend a lot of time noticing and examining our feelings, our thoughts, and our body sensations. There is much to be learned from such a practice. However, without a specific purpose it is usually best to let your thoughts, feelings, and sensations come up into awareness and then let them go. Generally speaking, outside of a focused exercise, there is no good purpose in becoming attached to them. The mind will produce a continuous series of thoughts, feelings, and sensations. That is what the mind does. Unless you attach importance to them, they will naturally disappear and be replaced by new thoughts, feelings, and sensations. When we are spending time examining our thoughts, feelings, and sensations it can become difficult to release them when the exercise is over. This meditation will help you to return to a normal state of allowing your thoughts, feelings, and sensations to flow through your mind.

To begin your meditation, sit in a comfortable position with your back straight to allow energy to flow freely through the chakras. Sit in a room where you will not be disturbed. Turn off your phone. Dim the lights or turn them off completely. Start by taking a big breath in and letting it out. Place one hand on your belly and one hand on your lower back. Breathe in deeply and feel your belly and lower back expand. Then release your breath and feel your belly and lower back compress. After two or three deep belly breaths, allow your breathing to return to normal. Place your hands on your thighs, palms down. Close your eyes if you haven't done so already.

Bring your attention to your breath – breathing in, breathing out. You will notice that thoughts, feelings, or sensations come into your mind. This is normal. Notice each one as it arises. Name it. For example, it may be a feeling: "happiness," or a thought: "did I let the dog in," or a sensation: "my back is itchy." As soon as you notice what your mind presents you, imagine a boat floating down a stream and place the thought, feeling, or sensation on the boat. Watch it continue down the stream and disappear.

Return your attention to your breath – breathing in, breathing out. Whenever you notice another feeling, thought, or sensation, place it on a boat and watch it float down the stream and disappear. Continue until the practice becomes automatic.

When you are ready to end your meditation, let go of your image of the boat and sit quietly with your eyes partially opened but focused on a spot on the ground a short distance in front of you. Count your breaths – breathe in, breathe out, one; breathe in, breathe out, two; etc. When you reach ten, open your eyes completely.

Chapter Six

ATONEMENT

Steps Eight and Nine in the traditional twelve-step programs deal with making amends. In Step Eight, you make a list of all persons you have harmed and become willing to make amends to them all. Then, in Step Nine, you make direct amends wherever possible, except when to do so would injure them or others. In Chapter Four, you looked back at your behavior during your active alcoholism and made a moral inventory. You have written down what you did, using the Five Precepts as your guide. And you discovered what the result of your behavior was – how it affected you and how it affected others. Clearly you harmed yourself during your active alcoholism. Put your own name at the top of the list of "all persons you have harmed."

Getting started by putting one name on your list is fairly simple. The difficulty comes in when trying to figure out what other names to put on your list. And then a multitude of questions arise. What does it mean to make amends? What is the difference between direct amends and indirect amends? How do you determine if making amends would further injure someone? These are questions that I struggled with in my recovery and every other recovering alcoholic I know has struggled with these questions as well. These questions merit some investigation.

Let's begin by looking at the word repent. The Oxford Canadian dictionary defines the word repent as "wishing you had not done something." As you read over your moral inventory, take your time. Stop after reading each event and look inside yourself. Remember that we are now in the Garden of Introspection. You are becoming very familiar with your body sensations, your thoughts, and your feelings. When you read an item on your moral inventory, do you notice a contraction or tug somewhere in your body? This is your body telling you there is unease with the situation.

When you remember the event you just read, do you feel ashamed, or bitter, or depressed, or embarrassed, or horrified, or numb, or shaky, or sorrowful, or unhappy, or worried? What do you feel? Name your feeling. Does the thought "I wish I hadn't done that" enter your head? If you answered yes, then you are probably experiencing repentance. But don't stop here! I have watched too many people stop at this point and then become consumed with guilt. There is no place for guilt in Buddhism. Let me repeat that: There is no place for guilt in Buddhism. The only reason we reflect on our past behavior is to learn from our mistakes.

Without acknowledging our responsibility in harming others, we will continue to carry the karma for that action. It is important to acknowledge your responsibility without making excuses or offering explanations. Karma is the natural result of the action. It is the law of cause and effect. Pre-Buddhist styles of karma involve reward and punishment. Post-Buddhist styles of karma do not. Try to be an objective observer of the situation. Did your action cause harm? Yes or no? Who did your action harm? Write down the name on your moral inventory. I find it helpful to use a pen with a different color of ink. Then at the end of this exercise, you can quickly scan your inventory and add the new names to your list of all persons you have harmed.

The first task in making a direct amend is to contact the person. A direct amend takes place face to face. Phone, text, or email the person and ask if you can meet with them in a public place like a coffee shop. You have harmed them in the past and they may not be comfortable except in a public area. It is possible that they will say no. I have not had this experience myself, but it is imperative that you respect their decision.

The purpose of the direct amend is to build a bridge, if possible, so the other person feels better. Your job is to name what you did and describe the circumstances. Next you acknowledge that you know that what you did caused them harm. You apologize for your actions. If you have stolen money or property you repay or return whatever was taken. You do not ask for forgiveness. You are there to help the other person heal. The focus is entirely on helping the other person feel better.

If you are not able to meet with the person you harmed, then you can make an indirect amend. Perhaps when you contacted the person they said no to your request for a meeting. Perhaps you live far away from one another and you have neither the time nor money to travel to where they live. Perhaps they have died. If you are unable to meet with the person directly, then an indirect amend is in order.

The most common form of indirect amend is a letter. You may think a text or email or phone call would suffice, but a written letter is your best option. This will be an emotional experience for the recipient. Allow them as much control over the situation as possible. Put your name on the return address. In this way, the recipient has the option to throw the letter out without reading it. That is their option. Your job is to write the letter. What the other person does with it is not your business. You can include your address, email, or phone number with the invitation to get in touch with you, if they wish. The choice is theirs. Because this will likely be emotional for the recipient, an actual physical piece of paper allows the experience to be more real.

If the person you harmed has died, you can still write them a letter. What would you say to them if they were still alive? Write it down. This is another occasion when a fire ritual can be useful. Once the letter has been completed, read it out loud as if the person were in front of you. Then burn the letter.

These direct and indirect amends are very important. By making these amends to specific people, you are repairing your past. You are "sweeping the dirt away." I have made both direct and indirect amends to people. I experienced a clear sense of freedom in every situation, regardless of the outcome with or for the other person.

I have also been the recipient of direct amends. I learned more from being on the receiving end. It allowed me to see more clearly what worked for the recipient and what didn't work. I have received several direct amends. Only one of them left me with a feeling of lightness and goodwill. I often think back to that experience and express my gratitude for it.

Before I tell you about that transforming experience, let me tell you what the other amends sounded like. Some were blanket expressions of regret "for everything I've done to you." Really? I'm guessing you're not even sure what it was you did when you are unable to name it. I'm left wondering if we are even thinking of the same event. No closure there. Other amends may name an event but then go on to explain why it happened. It could be blamed on something from their past. I'm left wondering if they are expecting sympathy from me. Some people have actually blamed their bad behavior on me. It goes something like this, "I'm really sorry I did x but you have to realize I only did x because you did y." It sounds like you are looking for an apology from me. This reversal of roles is not good. Clearly, there is no closure there.

These types of non-amends left me with a yucky feeling inside. But I learned from them. I do not want to impose that same yucky feeling on someone else. Especially on someone I have identified as a person I know I have harmed. I want only to try to repair that harm, not add to it.

I received a transformative amend early in my recovery and it allowed me to see the true beauty of what is possible. It came from a person with whom I had an on-again off-again relationship over a period of years. I had not seen him since I stopped drinking and entered recovery. One day I bumped into him on the street and he asked if we could find a place to chat. I was completely unprepared for what came next. He said he regretted the way our relationship had been in the past, that he knew he'd behaved badly and hurt me. He then went on to describe a few of those events. He expressed sorrow at his own past behavior, and he said he wanted to move forward with new behavior. He wanted us to be friends and promised to be only kind and helpful in the future. He asked if I'd be willing to let him try to be a better person.

His "confession" and his willingness to change had a profound effect on me. Although he had said nothing about my behavior, I was acutely aware of the wrongs I had done as well. I was very new in recovery and trying to change all kinds of behavior. Of course I was willing to try to change how we treated one another. I felt full of hope. Over the course of time I made direct amends to him as well. We were both able to move forward in our lives with kindness. It was a gift.

Such a gift is possible on the recovery path, on the Buddhist path. It is perhaps best illustrated by the Buddhist story of Kishimojin. This gift is made possible through compassion and wisdom.

Kishimojin lived in ancient India at the same time as Shakyamuni Buddha. She was a demon who transformed into a goddess. As a demon she lived in the hills with her children—all one hundred of them! She loved each of her children very much. In order to feed her many children she would sneak into the neighboring town during the night and steal a child from one of the homes. Then she would take this stolen child and feed it to her own children. The townspeople did not know what to do.

Eventually they went to the Buddha for advice. The Buddha agreed to help them. While Kishimojin was away from her own children in the night, the Buddha took one of her children and hid it. When Kishimojin returned, she noticed that one of her children was missing. She was extremely upset. She went to the Buddha to seek advice. The Buddha said to her, "If you are this upset over losing one of your children when you have so many, think how upset the townspeople are when they lose one child and they only have a few."

Kishimojin was able to put herself in the place of the townspeople. She understood for the first time that it was wrong to steal their children. She vowed to change her ways. She understood how painful it was for them to lose a child. She vowed to feed her own children pomegranates in the future and to protect all children from harm.

The Buddha taught Kishimojin compassion. Compassion is made up of two parts. The first is Ji, which means having empathy, being able to relate on a human level. The second part is Hi, which involves doing an action to end or remove the suffering. In Buddhist ethics, compassion is the dominant determinant in one's actions. We need to weigh all the factors in each specific situation. In order to do so, we must be able to put ourselves in another's shoes. This involves imagining yourself in their culture, in their gender, with their education, in their family situation, in all ways. When Kishimojin is able to imagine the pain and suffering of the parents from whom she stole children, she has compassion for them and she vows to change her behavior. She vows to stop causing pain and to give happiness by protecting the children from harm in the future.

It is this compassion that transforms her from a demon to a goddess and guides her life choices in the future. Every living being is capable of transformation. The vehicle is compassion mixed with wisdom.

Meditation For Compassion

Settle your body into a comfortable position for meditation. You may choose to sit on a cushion on the floor, sit on a chair, lie down, or stand in preparation for walking. As long as your spine is straight, any of these positions are fine. If you choose a walking meditation, then allow your eyes to become half-closed and softly focus your gaze downward and in front of you. If you choose a sitting or lying position, allow your eyes to gently close.

Begin your meditation by bringing your attention to your breath. Breathe in slowing, filling your chest and then your abdomen. Breathe out slowly, completely emptying your abdomen and chest. Take two or three more full, deep breaths in and out. Then allow your breath to return to a normal rhythm. Be aware of your breath without trying to control it in any way.

Place your hands over your heart center. Bring your attention to this area. Feel your chest rising and falling. Feel your heart beating. Imagine your heart pumping blood to all areas of your body. Imagine your blood circulating throughout your body and returning to your heart. Imagine that your heart is also radiating love and clarity. Love and clarity are circulating throughout your body, filling you with warmth and strength. Stay with this image for several minutes. Then, bring your awareness to the space surrounding your body. Can you feel the warmth and strength that is circulating within your body start to radiate outwards? Repeat the following phrases:

1. I see clearly the effects of my actions on myself.

2. I see clearly the effects of my actions on others.

3. I wish to end my suffering and the suffering of others.

4. I wish to send loving thoughts to myself and to others I have harmed.

5. I wish to treat myself and to treat others with kindness.

6. May it be so.

Repeat the phrases as often as you wish, then gently let them go. Return your attention to your breath. Softly open your eyes. Wiggle your fingers and toes and bring awareness to your body and your surroundings. When you feel ready, stretch, and leave your meditation.

THE THIRD GATE
THE DANCE OF LIFE

You will walk the Way to Buddhahood step by step, and finally become a Buddha in a good world.

(*The Lotus Sutra*, Chapter XIII, pg. 205)

Chapter Seven

FLOW

When you pass through the third gate, you are living your life by attending to each moment as it arises. The skills you learned in the Garden of Awareness and in the Garden of Introspection will serve you well as you move forward with your life. It is time to let go of your past. You do not need to forget your past, but you don't dwell on your past or place your focus there. The only time that really matters is this moment, right here, right now.

What does this moment, right here, right now, look like? The Buddha teaches that there are ten realms or worlds. Each of these worlds contains all of the others in potential. Our lives fluctuate from one to another. No matter what world you exist in in one moment, you have the potential to move to any other world in the next moment. Each moment is followed by another moment. Our experience in each moment is always changing. It is important to let go of any attachment to specific feelings or moments. Attachment is the primary problem of the alcoholic—chasing the high. On the other side of the coin is detachment or trying to avoid or run away from uncomfortable feelings or moments. Remember the technique of placing your uncomfortable feeling on an imaginary boat and letting it float away. Living in the present moment means allowing whatever is present to just be—not clinging to it or pushing it away. Truly knowing that nothing lasts forever, that everything in your world is in constant transition, is the basis of amazing good hope.

What are the ten worlds that we humans move around in? These ten worlds can be divided into two distinct realms, four in the enlightened realm and six in the unenlightened realm. Let's look at the unenlightened realm first. The basic natures of most people's lives are found there. We most often fluctuate among the worlds of Hell, Gaki, Animal, Asura, Human, and Heaven.

What is the world of Hell? Where does it exist? If you look back to the Gate of Awareness, this section of your path contains a quote from Nichiren Shonin. He says that Hell exists within five feet of our bodies. Hell is a state of mind. It is a place of agony and deepest suffering. You are in the world of Hell when you revisit and relive old painful experiences. You are in Hell when you cling to regret and refuse to allow forgiveness of yourself or others. You are in Hell when you are in extreme physical agony. Perhaps your pain is brought on by a disabling illness. Perhaps your pain is brought on by an injury to your body. Perhaps your pain is brought on by loss. Hell is the world of painful moments.

The Gaki world is the world of Hungry Spirits. Imagine gaunt ghosts or spirits devouring everything in sight. These hungry ghosts have very thin throats, as thin as a thread. Their bellies are swollen. They want and covet everything they see. Whatever they see becomes the focus of their desire and craving. But no matter how much they consume, they are never satisfied. They can never fill their swollen bellies. And when they do consume something and it makes its way down the long thread of throat, then it burns when it hits their belly. Their appetite is insatiable. No matter what the object of their desire, be it alcohol, drugs, food, gambling, shopping, or sex, there is no satisfaction. They suffer the desire, the craving, with no hope of ever satisfying the craving. They exist in a state of perpetual lack. This Gaki world is familiar to the active alcoholic, especially just prior to entering the recovery path. However, it can also reappear at any moment.

The Animal world is concerned with following only instincts. When you are in the Animal world, you are concerned primarily with issues around food, shelter, and safety. Fear is often a significant piece of the Animal world. Are you afraid that someone or something is going to take away your basic needs and that you will not be able to survive? The hunt for basic needs and the fear that they won't be found or that they will be taken away predominate in the Animal world.

The world of Asura is the world of anger. This is where you fight your demons. Someone has harmed you and you are unable to let it go. You are going to "make" them see what they did to you. You are going to even the score. The danger here is that you can easily become lost in the world of Asura. You walk around with a chip on your shoulder, full of resentments.

The up side of the world of Asura is that anger can also be a gift. It can provide the energy necessary to move out of sadness and depression. Perhaps you can use your anger to fuel your actions to support a cause to relieve similar suffering for other people. Many social justice causes are initially fueled by the anger behind personal or societal injustices. Instead of fighting your personal demons, you learn to fight injustice in order to relieve suffering for all humans.

The world of Humans is reflected in the conditions of everyday life. This includes your family life: family of origin and your own partner and children, your career or working life, your hobbies and the pursuit of your interests, your education (both formal and informal), your friendships, your travels, your spiritual life. The world of Humans is full and varied. What does your Human life look like? How many moments in your day are devoted to this world?

The Heavenly world is a place of peacefulness and contentment. At this point along your recovery path, you will have experienced some moments of peacefulness and contentment. They are wonderful moments. You might experience peacefulness and contentment when you are hiking in the wilderness, or canoeing on a river, or cross-country skiing in the mountains. You might experience peacefulness and contentment when you hold your child or grandchild for the first time, or when you pet your dog, or when you enter your temple. The experience that releases peacefulness and contentment will be different for different people. At first blush it appears ideal – something to strive for. Oh, oh. Did you catch it? Striving = craving = attachment. So subtle! This human mind is a trickster! There is an important difference between noticing that you are feeling peaceful and striving to create that feeling. The other danger within the Heavenly world is that contentment can too easily slide into laziness. The Heavenly world is very enticing, but be aware of the dangers it presents as well.

The next four worlds comprise the Enlightened Realms. The first three of these realms are called the three vehicles of enlightenment. Each world describes a different method or way of achieving enlightenment. The first of the Enlightened worlds is that of the Sravakas. These are the followers of the Buddha who lived in the same time as the Buddha and heard his teachings directly from the Buddha. Nichiren Shonin pointed out that we are all Sravakas when we study the Lotus Sutra.

The second Enlightened realm is that of the Prateka-buddha or "private Buddha." These seekers do not enlist a teacher. The goal is enlightenment for oneself only. They lead a secluded life, avoiding other people. The downfall or weakness of these seekers is self-centeredness. Without community, one cannot understand the interconnection of all things. Without community it is difficult, if not impossible, to develop compassion for others.

The third world in the Enlightened Realm is the world of the Bodhisattva. A Bodhisattva seeks enlightenment for oneself as well as for other sentient beings. A Bodhisattva is working in this world for the benefit of all beings, and is able to attain compassion and wisdom.

The Lotus Sutra teaches that these three enlightened vehicles/worlds are united in the one Buddha vehicle, the world of the Buddha. The Buddha's world is the world of the Buddha's enlightenment that he achieved while meditating under the Bodhi tree.

Awareness is the entry level for taking inventory. Practice awareness of your mental states throughout each day. Ask yourself which of the ten worlds you are operating in and become familiar with each. Notice and name the world without judging. Become curious.

Bring into your awareness a familiarity with body states as well. Notice if you feel a contraction in your gut, or a clenching of your jaw, or any other signals of tension in your body. Tension in your body is often a signal that something in your world is not right. Shoulders tense, belly tightens, and breathing gets shallow. This is usually a signal for defensiveness and anxiety. Be aware of the messages your body sends you. Investigate with curiosity.

Once you start to develop awareness and familiarity of both your mental states and your body signals, you will be able to reflect on your world and take an inventory. The purpose of an inventory is not so much to identify when you are "wrong." Rather you approach an inventory like a detective. You are gathering information. You want to discover what the effect of your feelings, bodily sensations, and actions is. You can then make a decision regarding how you might behave in the future if you are in a similar situation.

I take three different types of personal inventory. Different systems work for different people. I encourage you to try a variety of methods and choose the ones that work best for you.

The first type of inventory I do is a daily inventory. I do it twice a day – once in the morning and once late in the afternoon. I attach it to other activities I do on a daily basis so that it becomes automatic. I have a regular meditation practice and I chant in front of my Buddhist altar twice a day. I incorporate my daily inventory into these practices. First thing in the morning, after my chanting and silent mantra meditation, I do an inventory that is really more of an intention-setting practice. What do I want to see in the day ahead? Depending on what events I know are scheduled, I may ask for courage, or patience, or kindness. If there is nothing specific coming up for me in the day, I set an intention to give my body exercise, to give my mind challenges, to seek opportunities to be helpful, and to let go of troubling thoughts. It only takes a minute or two.

After my late afternoon chanting and meditation, I review my day to that point. Did I exercise my body? Did I challenge my mind? Did I find opportunities to be helpful? Did I let go of troubling thoughts? Chances are I have fallen down in at least one of these areas. If it is simply a problem of omission, I can set a goal to fulfill that particular intention before the day ends. Perhaps it is as simple as going for a walk after my dinner. If I discover I am hanging on to troubling thoughts, it is not quite so simple.

Did my troubling thoughts affect my behavior towards other people? Perhaps I will need to review my behavior with respect to the precepts. What action can I take to make the rest of my day more nourishing for myself and for others? I find this type of daily inventory helps to catch small irritations or patterns of behavior from growing.

The second type of inventory I use is a weekly inventory. If you choose to do a weekly inventory, decide which day works best for you and do it on the same day every week. It is so much easier to develop new behaviors if you are able to build in regularity. After doing several different types of inventories and awareness exercises, I noticed that a recurring problem for me is stress. Unchecked, it can lead to problems with insomnia, muscle tension, and digestive difficulties. I experienced all of these symptoms to the point where my daily life experiences were being severely impacted. If you begin to notice that you have one particular recurring problem, you may decide a weekly inventory is helpful.

My stress symptoms were huge by the time I took action. My first attempt at correcting the situation was to deal with each symptom individually. I learned everything I could about insomnia and instituted a sleep regimen, fine-tuning it till I was able to get a good night's sleep. I wore a mouth brace at night to relieve tension in my jaw, and went for massages to relieve built-up muscle tension in my body. I did a six-day body cleanse and re-introduced food types slowly. Once you identify the primary symptoms of your recurring problem, you will likely need to deal with direct relief of the symptoms as well.

However, the real work starts when you begin to reflect on what it is in your life that is contributing to this recurring problem. The fact that it is a recurring problem is a big clue to understanding that you are not dealing with your situation in a nourishing, healthy fashion. This is where a weekly inventory comes in very handy. Start to journal about your symptoms and make a note of what you are doing, what people you are with, what time of day it is, etc. Review your journal once a week and look for patterns. Stress is my biggest health problem. I can keep it in check quite easily by monitoring symptoms and situations on a weekly basis. An inventory of this type is designed to help you be the best version of yourself you can be.

The last type of inventory I take is a seasonal inventory. I live in a country, Canada, where there are four very distinct seasons. Winters are cold with snow; spring is muddy and heralds the return of flowers and birds; summer is hot and dry, and fall is so beautiful with the changing colors of the leaves and the sound of the geese on the river. There are certain activities that are restricted to a particular season. I can only go snow skiing in the winter. I can only plant a garden in the spring. I can only go canoeing or kayaking in the summer. I can only harvest my garden in the fall. My seasonal inventories are times of wish lists and goal setting. On the first day of each season, I think about the days ahead. What do I want this season to look like? Anything goes! Big dreams or little dreams – I write them down. Then I post my list of dreams in a place where I will see it every day and I try to let my dreams, my hopes, guide me. I don't treat it like a checklist. It is simply a gentle guide. Try it out and see if this kind of inventory provides you with inspiration.

Living a healthy lifestyle, without addiction, is not a guarantee that every moment will be peaceful and/or happy. That would be unrealistic. What you are learning is to identify what is going on in your world in any given moment. There is no need to stuff feelings or drown them with booze. Bring every experience into your awareness. Be honest with yourself and others about what is happening for you. Make nourishing choices for yourself. There will be times when you dance with joy. There will be other times when you dance with grief. Allow yourself to truly feel whatever is coming up for you in each moment. Make friends with your feelings and invite them to dance with you.

Chapter Eight

PRAYER AND MEDITATION

Prayer and meditation are foundational practices on my recovery path and on my Buddhist path. It is through prayer and meditation that the recovery path and the spiritual path become intertwined and the awareness emerges that there is only one path. It is through prayer and meditation that this truth is revealed. Our spiritual life is not separate from our everyday life. How we live every moment of every day is our expression of our spiritual life. I cannot knowingly harm myself or harm others without knowingly increasing suffering in this world. Clearly that would contradict the basic vow to relieve suffering for all sentient beings.

This step on the recovery path is especially important because it propels you into spiritual practices. A common question that I heard around AA recovery tables was "What's the difference between prayer and meditation?" If you google this question, you will get a variety of answers, depending on the spiritual tradition of the writer. I think it is an important question. Some people on the recovery path have no spiritual tradition. Others have abandoned the spiritual tradition of their childhood.

When I first entered recovery by going into a treatment center in the mid-1970s, I had no spiritual tradition. My introduction to spiritual practices was the Serenity Prayer. "Grant me the serenity to accept the things I cannot change, the courage to change the things I can, and the wisdom to know the difference." I believe this prayer is still widely used in recovery circles. It is a great starting point. Like other prayers, it is making a request using words. In this case it is a personal request for self. When you are new to recovery, the focus is necessarily on you.

Over the years, I investigated different spiritual practices. At one point I joined The United Church of Canada, but found it didn't quite fit with my spiritual experiences. I explored and practiced a variety of meditation practices. I found all of them helpful. At this point in my life, I am a practicing Nichiren Shu Buddhist.

I practice prayer and meditation on a daily basis. I will describe what I do, how I do it, what purpose it serves for me, and what benefits I derive from it. My practice has evolved over the years. If there is anything contained in my practice that you think would be beneficial for your spiritual journey, please try it out!

Every morning when I wake up, one of the first things I do is go to my home altar. I light a candle and then light incense using the flame from the candle. My home altar is set up in a particular fashion and I follow the Nichiren

Shu Dharma book regarding structure of a service. My morning service includes both prayer and meditation. The prayers I recite are contained within the Dharma book and are identified as prayers. They contain words that convey intention, or hope, or conviction, or wishes.

A prayer could be said for yourself. A personal prayer can be inserted into the general prayers in my morning service. Examples of personal prayers might be, "May I endeavor to increase connection and peacefulness at the family gathering this afternoon," or "May I have the strength and the courage to speak my truth throughout this day."

A prayer could be said for another specific person or being. Examples of prayers for others might be, "May Isabelle experience joy and good health throughout her pregnancy," or "May Ralph, my pet dog, be at ease as he recovers from his injury."

A prayer could be said for all beings. These prayers are written out in the Dharma book. Examples of prayers for all beings include:

1. May peace permeate the world and all beings enjoy peace and happiness!

2. May we purify our minds, limit our desires, learn to be content, feel free to experience the quiet unassuming joys of life, and learn to abandon all attachments formed in the mind!

A prayer could be said for the spirit of any being when they pass from this life. A personal prayer for the spirit of the recently deceased being is said each morning for seven days after someone passes from this life. Then once a week, each week, for seven weeks a prayer is again said for the spirit of the being who passed. A general prayer is said every morning for all the spirits of the universe.

I especially like starting my day with prayers. The prayers that are said every day remind me of the Buddhist vows I have taken and the commitment I have made to life. Active addiction is a turning away from life. Prayer returns me to the abundance of life. The individual prayers I insert on any given day help me to be mindful of what is coming up for me and for others. The afternoon service provides a gentle reminder on the days that go in a direction I hadn't anticipated. It helps me get back on track.

The prayers that I say in my home service are spoken aloud. Using my voice is a subtle but effective way of adding conviction to them. They are the only structured prayers I use.

I also use silent prayers throughout the course of my day. These are prayers I create depending on what I encounter. If I pass by a dead bird on my walk along the riverbank, I will say a silent prayer for the bird's spirit. If I see a family member or close friend in trouble of any kind, I will pray that they are able to come through their difficulty with ease. Depending on the world news of the day, I may say a silent prayer for peace in the world. I find that this practice of silent prayer helps me to pay more attention to what is going on around me and feel my connection to others and the interconnection of all beings.

Prayer has an important place in my life, but it is

through meditation that I gain access to my true essence, my "Buddha Nature." It is only through this type of spiritual experience that I made huge gains in insight and transformation. Don't get me wrong. I'm not claiming any kind of spiritual supremacy or mastery. I remain a human being stumbling my way through life. But I have had spiritual experiences and these spiritual experiences are the result of meditation. So let's talk about meditation.

There are many different types of meditation and there are many documented benefits of meditation. The primary difference between prayer and meditation is that meditation practices have the ability to take you to altered states of consciousness. Prayer is only employed in our waking state and because it uses meaningful language, it keeps us in our minds. Prayer is dependent on intellect to some degree. It is a goal-directed activity. Meditation takes us out of our mind. It is a centering practice.

My first experience with meditation was Transcendental Meditation when I was a teenager. I found it calming but never did develop a consistent meditation practice as a teenager. Later, when I entered treatment and recovery in my twenties, I was given the book, *The Relaxation Response*, written by Herbert Benson, M.D. I found this book fascinating. By this time in my life, I was experiencing stress and was familiar with the symptoms. I knew what the fight or flight response felt like. I could feel my heart pounding ferociously in my chest. My breathing would become faster. I would start sweating. I would clench my jaw and all my muscles in my body would tighten. It would become difficult to sit still. My thoughts would be racing. The physiological changes I was not aware of before reading the book include stress hormone release, shifting blood circulation away from digestion to muscles, stickier blood-clotting cells, and weakened immunity.

There was a time in our past when the fight or flight reaction made sense. If I was out hunting and a tiger jumped in front of me, these reactions would ready me to either fight the tiger or run away from the tiger. *The Relaxation Response* provided a documented method of countering the automatic effects of the flight or fight response. The documented method presented in the book is Transcendental Meditation. This was my introduction to the idea that a meditation practice would help someone who is experiencing stress. It could help me deal with my own stress overload!

Many more scientific studies have taken place since the 1970s that all show similar results. Perhaps the best known is the work of Jon Kabat-Zinn and his Mindfulness-Based Stress Reduction Programs at the Center For Mindfulness, UMass Medical School.

Reduction of stress was my entry point motivation for taking up meditation. It is the entry point for many people. Reduction of stress is one of the main reasons given for taking a meditation course. Reduction of stress is one of the main benefits of a meditation practice. You will get positive results whether you use mantra-based meditation or mindfulness meditation.

What is happening when you meditate that accounts for these kinds of changes in your body and your mind? The answer lies in the question. Stress is a reaction that occurs in both the body and the mind. They feed off of one another and the acceleration can easily lead to anxiety and/or panic. The way to interrupt the acceleration is to calm both the body and the mind. This is exactly what meditation does. The vehicle used is the breath. Meditation starts by asking you to sit in a comfortable position. The body is being taken care of. Then you are asked to take a deep breath in, all the way down to your belly. Perhaps you hold the breath for a few counts, and then you slowly release the breath. This counters the shallow breathing associated with stress. After a few deep breaths, you are asked to focus. In mantra-based meditation, you repeat your mantra. In mindfulness meditation, you will receive instruction to focus on your breath, or on one of your senses, or on something else depending on the teacher's training and background. Your racing thoughts start to slow down. Your body relaxes, your breathing slows, and your thoughts drift by. You enter the calm space of meditation.

A meditation practice will not take away stressful situations in your life. What it does is allow you to choose your reaction to stress. When there is less attention given to the negative elements of your life, you are able to enjoy more freedom of choice, more relaxed relationships and more creativity.

There are many guided meditations that can help to alleviate stress. Guided meditations are a bit of a hybrid between prayer and meditation. They are like meditation in that they start by getting you to position your body in a comfortable manner – either sitting, standing, or lying down. Then you are asked to pay attention to your breath. So, a guided meditation is part meditation in the way it helps you to calm your body and your mind first. Then it becomes somewhat like a prayer in that it employs specific words (language, not sounds or vibrations) with a specific purpose in mind.

In early recovery, I used a lot of guided meditations. I purchased CDs that had spoken meditations for mornings and for evenings, for chakra balancing, for stress reduction, and meditations for manifesting. Some of the people who created these CDs include Dr. Wayne Dyer, Dr. Deepak Chopra, Jon Kabat-Zinn, Thich Nhat Hanh, and Eckhart Tolle. I was part of an informal women's group that shared ideas about recovery practices. We would share CDs and anything else that any of us found useful. It was a supportive and helpful group.

Today it is not necessary to purchase CDs. There is an extremely helpful, free app called "Insight Timer" that you can put on your phone or laptop. It contains a wide selection of guided meditations. The categories it includes are self-love, pregnancy and parenting, inner peace, sleep, acceptance, stress, mornings, emotional balance, mindful eating, movement, mindfulness, relax, gratitude, and recovery. The recovery category includes recovery from addiction, trauma, or illness. I strongly encourage you to try some of these out.

Guided meditations have structure. There are other forms of structured meditations as well. You again start by calming your body, usually using a specific sitting position. You will calm your mind, usually focusing on your breath.

Then you will introduce a series of thoughts in the form of silent sentences. The most common structured meditation that I use is the Loving-Kindness meditation you learned in Chapter Six. It is easy to modify to help you deal with any bothersome feeling or situation.

I asked my Buddhist minister, my sensei, what the difference is between a meditation like loving-kindness and the chanting meditation we do as Nichiren Shu Buddhists. I found his answer very helpful in understanding the different types of meditation, and the different purposes of meditation. A guided meditation or a structured meditation is very useful if you are dealing with a specific bothersome feeling or situation. But that is all it does. It treats a specific symptom.

Mantra-based meditations include the chanting meditation we do as Nichiren Shu Buddhists, and the Primordial Sound Meditation I learned at The Chopra Center, and Transcendental Meditation that I learned as a teenager. All of these forms of meditation rely on the vibration of particular sounds. Each of them has the ability to take you to your innermost self, to your "Buddha Nature." This is your essential self. Dr. Deepak Chopra calls this Unified Consciousness.

By tapping into our "Buddha Nature" during chanting or other mantra-based silent meditation practices, we are able to grow our "Buddha Nature." As you grow your "Buddha Nature," there is less and less room for troublesome thoughts or feelings. You become less reactive to specific situations and people. You see the bigger picture. You no longer see yourself as a separate being.

The chanting service in which I experience this the strongest is called "Shodai Gyo Meditation." It is the most beautiful and powerful service I have ever participated in. You are led into a meditative state by showing respect for the place of worship, showing devotion to the Buddha, the dharma, and our founder, Nichiren Shonin. A prayer is offered, followed by silent meditation to purify the mind and body. Then the leader begins the chanting of the Odaimoku: Namu Myoho Renge Kyo. The speed at which you chant varies, with the beat being kept through drumming. The volume at which you chant varies. Sometimes I feel great excitement with the chanting; sometimes I feel great connection, sometimes I simply lose any sense of self. There is another period of silent meditation after the chanting to reflect on the merits of the Odaimoku. A prayer is said, followed by the Four Great Vows, and the service ends. It is a profound experience. If ever you have the opportunity to participate, do so!

Prayer and meditation are foundational in recovery. Prayers can be said for yourself, for others, for all people, and for spirits that have passed from this world. They can be prayers you are taught, like the Serenity Prayer, or prayers you create yourself to meet situations in your life as they arise. Meditation has many benefits. When I teach meditation to others, I am often asked, "How do I know I am doing it right?" The answer is not found by looking at your experience while meditating. The benefits are seen in how you live your life.

Meditation has physiological benefits, psychological benefits, and spiritual benefits. Specific benefits include peace of mind, reduced stress, less anxiety, enlightenment, deeper connection to your "Buddha Nature," awakened creativity, more restful sleep, easing of pain, boosts the immune system, and allows for deeper, more loving relationships. If you meditate regularly, you will experience at least some of the many benefits of meditation. It is not unusual for others to notice these differences before you do. If friends or family members comment that you seem happier, more rested, less anxious, etc., they are reflecting back to you the changes they see. When you develop a regular meditation practice, your life improves.

Chapter Nine

OPENING THE MIND AND HEART TO LOVE

Step Twelve in the traditional AA program reads, "Having had a spiritual awakening as the result of these steps, we tried to carry this message to others, and to practice these principles in all our affairs." It is through prayer and meditation that we experienced a spiritual awakening. We awakened to our true essence, our "Buddha Nature." But this awakening also awakens the reality of our connection with all other beings. We live in an interconnected reality. What does that mean?

In the Lotus Sutra, the Buddha tells us the parable of the Magic City to help us grasp the implications of a fully lived human life. The parable begins by telling us of a remote place, a place where wild beasts and other dangers abound. There is a road that winds through this remote and dangerous place. To travel this road is a long and perilous trip. But many people want to travel the road because it leads to a land of riches, of treasures beyond description. There is a wise man that has traveled the road to the land of riches. He knows the twists and turns in the road very well. He agrees to lead a group of people on the road and take them to the land of treasure.

Many days and nights pass. The people become tired and discouraged. They wonder if perhaps it was a mistake to embark on this journey and some suggest they should turn back. They are on the brink of giving up. The wise leader, however, knows that if they carry on it is only a short distance further along the road before they reach their destination. In order to give the group the rest they so desperately need, the wise leader creates a vision, a magic city that they can all see just ahead. The people enter the magic city. They are safe. They are uplifted. They rest.

When the wise leader sees that the people are rested, he tells them that the city is an illusion that he created for them. The magic city vanishes. But now that they are rested there is no thought of turning back. The people know they are close to the land of treasure and they forge ahead with renewed enthusiasm. The group is brought safely to the treasure land.

The road through the remote land represents the road of life that each of us travels. Our lives can seem long and difficult. We can encounter hardships and pain (the wild beasts). The road of life doesn't always unfold in the manner we thought it would. There are twists and turns in the road and it is difficult to see where it is leading. This is especially true for those of us who struggled with alcohol addiction. Many humans become discouraged on the road of life and want to give up. They might become cynical or self-seeking or return to drinking. But giving up will not bring you the fullness of life, the treasure at the end of the road.

The parable teaches us how to carry on. The first thing to notice is that it is not a solitary trip. The journey in the parable is undertaken by a large group of people. We are social animals and community is important. Addiction leads you into a solitary existence. Recovery brings you into community. The abundance of life is found with others: your sangha, your recovery support group, your family, your friends, and your co-workers. You are not alone in the Garden of the Lotus Sutra. You are dancing with many others.

The travelers in the parable do not start out on their journey and simply hope for the best. They have a guide, a wise leader who has traveled the path before and knows the way. Look for wise leaders who have traveled the path you are embarking on. Seek guidance from them, especially when you feel discouraged. In early recovery, this guide was likely your addiction counselor or perhaps a sober person you admired. In the Garden of the Lotus Sutra, you will find a spiritual leader. My meditation practice led me into Buddhism where I found my sensei, my Buddhist minister. Trust your intuition. You will find your own wise leader.

When you are feeling tired and discouraged, remind yourself that all is not as it appears. You have used meditation to tap into the true essence of life, your "Buddha Nature." This human life we perceive with our senses is an illusion. We can return to our true essence any time we choose and gain rest and energy.

Being able to rest and renew ourselves through meditation is an exceptional skill. However, the peaceful land of meditation is not our destination any more than the Magic City was the final destination of the travelers in the parable. Once rested, they returned to the road and traveled on to the land of treasures. On our road through life, we may need to stop and rest from time to time. But then we return to the road of life until we reach our treasure land, the world of the bodhisattva.

In the world of the bodhisattva, you will recognize and use your innate talents and creativity in order to add happiness to your own life and to the lives of others. In this way, your human life becomes meaningful. The mind opens to all kinds of possibilities and the heart opens to all those who suffer. This is the treasure land, the Garden of the Lotus Sutra. Our destination, as humans, is full and abundant living in harmony with all others.

Full and abundant living involves inclining the mind towards wholesome mind-states. It is there that we will find the principles that guide us in this human life. These principles, these wholesome mind-states include, but are not limited to, the following: honesty, truth, acceptance, hope, commitment, willingness, courage, integrity, humility, love, reflection, justice, forgiveness, perseverance, vigilance, service, wisdom, compassion, responsibility, freedom, respect, generosity, joy, delight, and happiness.

It is my wish that in reading this book, you may be able to bring sobriety and the fullness of life into your world. May it be so.

WORKS CITED

Books

1. Alcoholics Anonymous, World Services, Inc., New York City, 1955

2. Nonviolent Communication: A Language of Life, Marshall Rosenberg, 2005

3. The Lotus Sutra, translated by Reverend Senchu Murano, 1974

Booklet

1. Essentials of Nonviolent Communication, Rachelle Lamb

Audio Tape

1. Self-Relaxation Training, Sherwin B. Coulter & Julio J. Guerra, 1976

Video

1. 3 Happiness Myths Debunked, Robert Holden, Hay House online learning

Activity Cards

1. Grok, Christine King & Jean Morrison, nvcproducts.com

Manufactured by Amazon.ca
Acheson, AB